50 EYEWITNESS DRAMAS
ON BIBLE TIMES

*To Sylvia, Mike and Phil
for being the most gracious critics*

50 Eyewitness Dramas on Bible Times

JOHN SPENCE

David C Cook®

transforming lives together

50 EYEWITNESS DRAMAS ON BIBLE TIMES
Published by David C. Cook
Kingsway Communications LTD
Lottbridge Drove, Eastbourne BN23 6NT, England

David C. Cook
4050 Lee Vance View, Colorado Springs, CO 80918 U.S.A.

David C. Cook Distribution Canada
55 Woodslee Avenue, Paris, Ontario, Canada N3L 3E5

The Web site addresses recommended throughout this book are offered
as a resource to you. These Web sites are not intended in any way
to be or imply an endorsement on the part of David C. Cook,
nor do we vouch for their content.

Unless otherwise stated Bible quotations are from the New International
Version © 1973, 1978, 1984 by the International Bible Society.

ISBN 978 1 842912 82 9

Cover design by ccdgroup.co.uk

Printed in the USA
First Edition 2007

1 2 3 4 5 6 7 8 9 10

Contents

Explanatory Note

These monologues have been grouped into either themes or events. They are not action pieces but serve rather to allow the characters to talk about a subject or event, while at the same time almost inadvertently to reveal something about their character. Many of them only really work if different people perform one each from the same set at the same event, the idea being to build up a picture of the incident. However, some of them also work as stand-alone pieces.

The backstories are there for biblical and historical context, or are a brief comment from me or from a character related to the main story (who may not feature in any of the monologues), or even from the actual characters themselves. These are designed to help the reader to fill out the character portrayed in the monologue.

Performance and Copyright

A note from the publisher

The right to perform sketches in this book is included in the price, provided that such performances are made within an amateur context, for example worship or education. Where any charge is made to audiences, permission in writing must be obtained from the author, who can be contacted care of the publisher, and a fee may be payable for the right to do so.

Please note that the text of this book is copyright, and that no part may be copied without permission from the publisher. Where multiple copies of a sketch are required for those playing the parts, it is generally simpler and better value to buy extra copies of the book.

However, where you have already purchased sufficient books but merely want to make a few paper copies for ease of use, please feel free to do so, destroying the photocopies when finished, so that they cannot be replicated elsewhere.

Thank you for your kind co-operation.

The Flood

The entire extraordinary story of the Flood can be found in Genesis 6–9. In a recent programme about the Flood, the BBC told of several epics that mention a Sumerian king who survived a massive flood in Mesopotamia. The story is supported by geological evidence of flooding in the area around 5,000 years ago. They asked, 'Could this story have provided the inspiration for the Jewish priests who wrote the book of Genesis 2,000 years later?' The BBC journalist Jeremy Bowen says: 'When they first heard the story, how could they fail to recognise its moral power? If humankind falls short of God's laws, there's a dreadful price to pay. Behind that moral message lies one of the world's greatest stories.' It is my belief that actually the Sumerian epics were based on the real Noah's story.

1 A villager

BACKSTORY

Villager's sister: 'My brother was killed visiting a girl in another village. In all, about half of my family have died in fights, most of them with people from outside the village. Heartache is a part of life. That's all there is to it. My sister has got friendly with the nutty woman whose husband is building that boat outside the village. She says they talk about her god a lot. Obviously there's no such thing. Everyone knows that. But this insanity is getting to her. If she's not careful, this idea from outside the village will take over her life and destroy the village values in her as surely as some man from outside the village killed our brother.'

MONOLOGUE

They've always lived here. Just a bit down the road from the village. Where the road dips, just by that big outcrop of rock. 'The Tusks,' Nate calls it. He reckons those two big spikes make it look like an elephant's face. Kids have got such imaginations.

Anyhow, they were living down there before I was born. I always think of them as hermits, a whole family of hermits. You never see him in the village. She comes sometimes, mainly to buy stuff at market. We have a chat occasionally. She's all right, whatever anyone tells you.

When Nate was little, we used to talk sometimes about family. She's got some strange views about family. Reckons you're only supposed to have one. Says she doesn't hold with men getting other men's women or women swapping homes. But apart from that she's quite normal. Actually said some useful things about how to handle Nate.

But her husband – Noah, I think his name is – spends all his energy these days on that enormous boat he and his sons are building. People say that he reckons a god told him to build it.

For the life of me, I can't figure what he thinks he's going to do with it. Why, even the nearest decent-sized lake must be almost 50 miles from here! And what would you do with it, even if you got it there?

And it's over 500 miles to the sea. And even then, what normal person floats a boat on the sea? And what normal use can there be in having a boat half the size of the village?

No. No two ways about it, he's seriously weird. The folks in the village say that when he was a youth he used to stand in the marketplace and preach. Used to say outrageous things, like there was only one god. And they say he used to get right passionate about it. Used to say that his god would destroy us all unless we changed our ways. Said we had to get rid of all our idols, close the brothels, take responsibility for our kids. Half the time I forget how many I've even had. All the village kids run about together. Who's to say which is which and who is who? Weird, I tell you. Weird.

Makes you wonder what she sees in him. I asked her once, but she didn't say much. Her world is so different from mine. She talks another language. Oh, it has the same words as ours, but they all seem to mean something else.

She said, 'He's my husband', like that should mean something to me. Said that she's going to be with him for life. She even said he's the father of her kids. I mean, how does she know? Unless she's only been with him. How weird would that be? And she said he doesn't have any other kids with any other women in the village. You know, I almost believe that. When does he get time? Too busy making that boat for his god.

That said, sometimes I do envy her. Envy her certainty. Even envy the way she does family. She reckons she really loves them, even her sons. (Mind you, she can list them all. She's only got those three.) And she says they love her. Talks about getting respect off those boys and tenderness off that weirdo of a man. Even after all this time.

I asked her about all this god business, and she reckons she really believes it too. Only one god. And she says that he – she's adamant about it being a him – she says that he tells them how to live. Fancy. Having someone in charge of you like that. And she says he loves them. She even says that he loves us.

I'm not sure he loves me. I'm not sure anyone really loves me like that. For life.

Do you think you can really know if anyone loves you? I'm not even sure what it means, that a god can love a person.

She says that he made us. All of us, even the other tribes. Says that all of us must answer to him – like, explain ourselves and all that. She says the way we all live is wrong, and it's upsetting him. And we can't count on him being patient forever. She watered up at that bit. Don't know why. She said something about a day of reckoning unless we all change. Said we should all be like her and Noah.

I can't ever see that happening. Mind you, she's so sure and so peaceful. I envy her that.

A couple of times I've had the strangest feeling. Like there being someone else in the room even when I know I'm alone, watching me, even trying to talk to me. Now, she would have said that was her god.

But it seems an awful big thing to change your whole life for a few feelings. At the end of the day, we've all got our own point of view.

2 Noah's wife

BACKSTORY

Scripture (2 Peter 2:5–10) speaks about the godly who lived in ungodly times before dramatic acts of judgement. It says about one of them that he was righteous, and that he was distressed by the filthy lives of lawless men and tormented in his righteous soul by the lawless deeds he saw and heard. Such a description would also fit Noah's wife.

MONOLOGUE

I suppose anyone might think our way of life is strange. Actually, *I* think it's strange.

Living in a world that's racing towards its own end. And not being able to make any of them stop and listen. But you still go to shop in the market. For fruit and stuff.

'Can I have a bag of apples and one of raisins? And by the way, did I mention that God is about to drown you all for being so persistently wicked?'

You can't say it like that. Noah says there's no point in trying to say it at all. Mind you, he tried harder than me or the boys at first. And where did it get him? Laughed at. Called a weirdo. Spat at. Even beaten up a few times – quite a few times, when he used to preach down in the market.

That's where I first saw him – preaching his heart out down in the market.

I thought he was magnificent even then. He used to have long hair in those days – thick, black, long hair. And he was so muscular. Actually, he still is. Lost all that hair, though. He says it's all the worry I give him. I used to say he had a cute bum. No, I didn't used to *say* that. I used to *think* it. I didn't really know him that well in those days.

It was a while before he noticed me. I used to meet him in the market and talk all the way home. He was the only other person I knew that wanted to see people turning back to God. And it grew to be a passion with us both.

And then one day he asked me to marry him. Out of the blue. One of the women in the village was asking me the other day about how we came to get married. She asked me if I would have married him if I had known about all the trouble his preaching would bring on us. I said yes, but I might not have married him if I had known he was going to lose all his lovely hair!

She laughed, but I don't think she really understood. It's as though she thinks of our faith and this ark as some kind of bizarre hobby. I've tried to tell her, but she never seems to get it.

At first Noah used to implore people to listen, but even then most of them just used to heckle.

'What's the use in only having one god? What if you lose it? What if it gets broken? The bloke over the road from me had four of his stolen.'

He would try so hard to make them see. 'God is awesome, powerful as a hurricane, gentle as a dove, not one of your tacky, tawdry little idols. Think about it! You used half that tree trunk for firewood. So how can the other half be

God? Use the brain God gave you! You don't look like you need a check-up from the neck up. Look around you! Who do you think made all this? Not that tin pot of a god you keep under the bed, that's for sure.'

But to no avail. Sometimes he could be so powerful, preaching as if he was wielding a sword, demolishing their arguments and mockery. Sometimes he was so passionate that I even saw the people listening to him moved to tears. But in the end nothing changed.

So God told him to start building an ark. And now that's pretty much all we do. Noah and our sons working on the construction. Me and the girls gathering and packing the supplies. One big evacuation project. Only it's not like trying to escape from a locust plague or a forest fire, with everyone pulling together. This time we're on our own, the entire world going on around us, quite oblivious to everything we've said, quite oblivious to whatever is coming next.

Sometimes it makes me tearful. Sometimes it makes me angry. How can they all be so blind? Most of the time it just makes me love them all the more. But I don't think that'll be enough.

3 Japheth

BACKSTORY

In 2 Peter 2:5 it says that God 'protected Noah, a preacher of righteousness, and seven others'. When we think of the Flood we usually think of Noah. This is the story of one of the seven others.

MONOLOGUE

It's not what I expected.

Just rain. A bit heavy, but basically rain. No writing in the sky. No thunderous voice from heaven. Not even an earthquake. Just rain.

I mean, we've seen more than enough miracles. All those creatures just coming to the yard – we weren't expecting that. It's been alternately funny and eerie. Every day, looking out the window to see a new set of animals. Even though we worked out why they were coming, it's still been bizarre. I mean, you don't expect it – a menagerie lurking outside your door.

And we've seen numerous instances of supernatural intervention – provision of tools and supplies of food, even the times when members of the family have recovered from illness when we've prayed. And then there is the undeniable fact of this ark, built at God's command. I mean, we couldn't have dreamt it up.

And now the rain. I know this is the beginning. By night it will be driving rain. Within a couple of days things will start to get washed away. Within a week some people will be trapped in their homes. Several will have drowned, trying to get to safety. Soon there will be no safety. People will be evacuating, unaware that shortly there will be nowhere to evacuate to. Nowhere to run.

But there's been no trumpet sound, no heavenly reverberation, no impact, no shock. We've been saying it for years, but no one believed us. Oh, a minority were interested, a few were intrigued, a handful were even disturbed. But no one thought it warranted building an ark of their own. It just never felt like a priority.

And now it's raining.

I don't feel anything, or rather, I feel so many different things that they all seem to cancel each other out.

I just saw the door to the ark close. None of us closed it – it just shut. One more miracle. One more mercy. If God hadn't chosen to caution us against wickedness, and then warn us of the impending flood, and finally to act, holding back the rain from us by securing that door, we would have drowned like all the rest.

And that clinches it. If God has shut us in, then I was right just now. This is the beginning.

An hour ago I was outside. I don't know when I'll be able to say that next. I don't really know if I'll ever be able to say that again.

I was walking back from the market. Just fancied buying some fruit. On the way back I met Mark. He'd just come back from working in the fields. Left all his tools outside the house and had just come back out to gather them up and take them in from the rain. He's like that, is Mark. Always wants things to be right. Leaving his tools outside in the rain would bother him. Might go rusty. Thing is, he hasn't worked it out yet, that it won't matter in a week or two, 'cos there'll be no one left to care. He'll be gone. His shrew of a wife'll be gone. His half-witted brother, his fastidious mum, his rather tarty sister – all gone.

In a lot of ways things have been 'business as usual' here, even in recent weeks – people eating, drinking, marrying, building houses same as ever. I know we've told them often enough. I know that they think we're just cranks. But I couldn't fight an overwhelming need to tell Mark just one more time.

'Just on my way back to the ark,' I said. 'Do you fancy a stroll? No? OK, but this is your last chance. We'll be sailing off in a few days. . . Yes, I know it's on dry land now, but we'll be afloat by the end of the week. Mark, I know you can't see how, but just believe me. Come with me. No, you can't "pop over" next week. There won't be a next week. This is your moment to repent, to put your faith in my God. It doesn't matter if you think you're as good as I am. Maybe you are. But I won't be spared by being good. I will be spared because I'll be inside a boat. It's as simple as that. I believe God, so I'm going to make sure I am on that ark in the next hour. That's the only way any of us will survive. If I'm not on it, I'll drown. If my brothers aren't on it, they'll drown. Even my wife, even my mum and dad. If they're not on it, they'll drown. And if you're not on it, you'll drown.'

But it was like scattering seed in a drought. Nothing sank in. So I walked back alone. And now I'm shut in the ark. All eight of us, Mum and Dad, me, my brothers, our wives – this is the new humanity now. I believe we will survive. God hasn't brought us this far to let it all go wrong.

Turning the World on its Head

Reading the whole story in Genesis 37–45 will give you the background to these scripts.

Joseph's brothers have had enough of him and sell him to slave traders. The slave traders take him to Egypt and sell him to Potiphar, the captain of Pharaoh's guard. Joseph stands out because of God's blessing, which results in Potiphar putting him in charge of his household. Potiphar's wife also notices Joseph, but with more amorous things in mind. One day she approaches him, but he refuses to be with her. He is then falsely accused of harming her and is thrown into prison. There he meets the Pharaoh's baker and cupbearer, whose dreams he interprets. The cupbearer is released, and somewhat later Joseph is also released, because Pharaoh needs him to interpret a dream of his own. He does this and is put in charge of the whole country. Later he is reunited with his brothers.

4 Joseph – the trial

BACKSTORY

Potiphar: 'Betrayal? Well, that's a question for the court, who will of course have as their prime consideration a wish to avoid embarrassing me. But I know what's worse. It's ill-timed. I trusted him with everything I've got. I put him in charge of the lot, both all my lands and everything in my house. He was doing a brilliant job of running the whole show. I did not have to think about anything except what to eat. But now I have other worries. My wife says he did it. It's not really a question of trivial things like facts; more to do with appearance. But it's going to be mighty in-convenient.'

MONOLOGUE

I have just been standing on holy ground. I know it. As surely as I live, I know I have been in the presence of God in a special way. I felt as Abraham must have felt when the Lord appeared as a burning brazier, or as my father Jacob must have felt when the angel of God wrestled with him one night and forever changed the way he walked.

Only they were alone before God. It was all very personal to them. No observers. Just the man and his God. And that has always appealed to something in me.

I have known moments like that. When my brothers dropped me in a well, that was a moment like that. God wrestled with me that day. Oh, it wasn't a physical presence like my father's angel, but it was every bit as real, every bit as personal, and yes, it changed the way that I walked through life. I was a gentler man from that day. My soul was quieter, less arrogant, less demanding. I met God alone in that well. Abandoned, betrayed, hopeless and, as I thought, about to die, I met God.

Many a day I have felt I would willingly go back to that well, just for the experience I had of God that day. No one can teach you that.

But today I met him in a different way. Once again my life was in question. But this time the voices I could hear weren't the muffled voices of my brothers as they planned what to do with me. No. They were the voices of my accusers, right here with me in the room.

I never thought I would be put on trial. I haven't done anything. And the charge is trumped up – my master's wife accusing me of assault, and worse. And there was nothing I could say.

Such things always bring grief, and grief upon grief. It brought back horrible memories of what happened to my sister Dinah.

I was only very young at the time, but I knew something was wrong. All I understood back then was that a man had hurt her and made her very sad. I remember her crying all the time, and a lot of shouting between my brothers and my father. And just when I thought peace had returned to the home, it all started again. Suddenly my father made us all become nomads again. My brothers had exacted a cruel revenge on the man who hurt my sister and had killed him.

But not him only. Simeon and Levi killed his father, every man in his family and every man in the town where he lived. My other brothers just looted the place. And now we had to flee to avoid further conflict.

It was hard. Deborah, who had been companion to my father's wife, and like an aunt to me, died on the journey. And then my mother died giving birth to my little brother. I only have vague childhood memories of how life was before all the trouble. It always seemed to me that what happened to Dinah lay at the root of all our unhappiness.

I still miss Mum. And I think her death made my father a lot more unhappy. Every year at the anniversary of her death he gets so tearful and withdrawn. Sometimes I used to think that my brothers didn't seem to notice. They just seemed to treat him as though he was incidental to their plans.

I wonder if he's still alive now.

What that man did to Dinah was an evil crime, and it brought more evil in its wake. And here I was, accused of the same thing by a woman who felt she had been spurned by me, and wasn't used to not taking anything she wanted. After all, she was wife to the mighty Potiphar, who was one of the most powerful men in the land and my master.

I was a little slow realising at first. She was my master's wife. What could be more natural than her taking an interest in what I was doing for him? She used to get me to explain all of his business affairs, always looking impressed at my efforts, always laughing at my jokes.

And then one day she said, 'I'm bored with this now. Take me out for a walk.'

It's not at all overtly immoral, but in my heart I knew it was an invitation to cross a line. After that she got progressively more blatant, and I got progressively more uncomfortable with the times she asked me to explain her husband's business matters.

And what made matters worse is that I was flattered and I was lonely. And she is strikingly eye-catching. But I have seen how the human heart plays tricks. You can convince yourself that it is all innocent by pretending to be humble, saying, 'Of course she couldn't be interested in a mere slave in *that* way', and suddenly it can seem almost spiritual to 'accidentally' flirt with a woman that God's law has put firmly off limits.

Well, I knew what lay ahead if I started down that way, and I didn't want to go there. But she obviously did. The more I made excuses not to be with her, the more she contrived to be with me. At first it was just the way she dressed that became more provocative. Then she found reasons to accidentally brush fingertips, sometimes even 'inadvertently' fall against me. Till in the end she said, 'We can't keep fighting the way we feel forever. Come to bed with me.'

And when I told her no, that it would be a betrayal of my God, and the man who had become both master and friend, I actually believe she was genuinely surprised. She had really convinced herself that she knew how I was feeling. At first she behaved hurt, but that soon turned to anger, and then contempt. How could I, a miserable slave, refuse her, one of the most powerful and attractive women in the land? Didn't I know how many men would risk death just to be noticed by her?

So now she stood in the room, attributing filthy words and filthy deeds to me. And no one would let me speak because of what she said I had done.

I don't think Potiphar really believed it. He had never said anything, but I used to see the look on his face when he came back unexpectedly and disturbed her attempts to flirt. If he had really believed her I would have been sent to my death instead of sent to a dungeon. But what could he do? He simply couldn't be seen to have even considered that a slave's word was worth more than his wife's.

And everyone else in the room had their own agenda. I had been my master's choice, the favoured servant. Most of them wanted me gone. And my friends were too scared to speak up for me. So I was mocked and vilified, accused of all manner of crimes.

They said I had schemed, worked my way to gain advantage and privilege, and watched for a moment when I could cruelly use my master's favour to abuse his wife. No one stepped forward for me.

I felt more alone, more betrayed than even when my brothers sold me as a slave. Such false accusations divest you of a sense of self-respect even as the others around you appear to agree with the allegations.

Was this what had become of the dream I had, when all my family gathered around me and bowed down to me? I realised way back when I was sold as a slave that the dream didn't promise me the right to lord it over them. But that things should come to this!

I was almost glad my father must already have given me up for dead long ago. I'm glad he wasn't there to see what I have been brought to.

I wasn't even allowed to speak in my own defence, was forced to listen as I was maligned and parodied and finally told that I would live out the remainder of my days in a squalid prison. Potiphar's wife even spat at me.

But just when I thought I could stand no more shame, God came to me. Somehow he is here, and he is working out his purpose in this shame.

At that moment, I realised that the true measure of a man is what he can endure, and what he can forgive. God came so close to my heart, I felt ennobled. I felt his objectives, his intention somehow unfolding in me. And I felt so loved.

Somehow it seems to me that he esteems those who believe his word and choose his purposes. He applauds us when we line up our lives with his intentions, but that's not why he loves us. His love felt so powerful at that moment that it made me feel liberated, realising that his purpose is so much greater than I am. I wanted to shout, 'It doesn't matter! He loves me. And all of us are powerless to stop him.'

So now I am on my way to prison, uncertain of what the future holds for me, but certain of who holds the future for me.

5 The chief cupbearer

Prisoner: 'Perhaps if that cupbearer had paid more attention to his own life, he might have noticed what that butler was doing behind his back. Then he wouldn't have got sent here in the first place. But the funniest thing I've heard was when Joseph asked the cupbearer to remember him when he got out of prison. Might as well have asked the sun not to shine! OK, so any chance of life, freedom and happiness for Joseph depended on him remembering. So – nothing important, then!'

MONOLOGUE

Yes, obviously I remember Joseph now, or should I say Zaphenath-Paneah. Of course I remember him now.

He was that rather serious, scrawny-looking man that the prison warder used as a way of keeping order in the prison, even though he was a prisoner himself. You see, they each had a theory about prison life.

Joseph's theory was that seeing as a man in prison will always think that it's unjust that he's there, and seeing as this leads to being overcome by helplessness and despair, and seeing as how those feelings often give way to frustration, anger, violence and general mayhem. . . seeing as all of this follows like night follows day, it figures that if you give the prisoner something useful and rewarding to do instead, you can break that destructive cycle. That was his theory.

The prison warder had a different theory. His theory was that if he could get Joseph to run the prison for him, then he wouldn't ever have to get off his fat backside and do anything even approximating to real work.

Happily, although they're very different theories, they complement each other with a harmony that's almost poetic.

So Joseph became assistant vice prison warder, leaving the real prison warder to get on with some real vice. Which was a big improvement on his way of doing things before Joseph came, namely extorting large sums of money, or on occasion some very dubious personal favours, out of prisoners' friends and family in return for giving the prisoners food instead of hanging them upside down by their feet.

I know all this because I spent a few months in there myself. Luckily, this was after Joseph got put in charge, which was just as well, as my family are always pretty broke, and I don't think my sister would have been at all keen on doing any dubious personal favours. And I don't think I would have enjoyed life as a bat.

I had been sent to prison over a misunderstanding in Pharaoh's household. Prior to that I had been his chief cup-bearer, which actually is what I am doing again now. Nice work if you can get it. It doesn't pay that well, but Pharaoh always was a tight-fisted oik, which is actually how I came to be in prison in the first place.

Remember how I said that every man in prison will think he's been a victim of some injustice? Well, in my case I really was. I got sent there with the baker on account of a mix-up over a consignment of very fine wine. For some reason the baker got it into his head that Pharaoh wouldn't mind if he drank a bottle, or two, or three, or even a whole case. And he was quite surprised when Pharaoh got upset over a whole missing case. Who could have known? I'll tell you. There's a lad in our village who's a bit simple, and he's a blind-mute, but even he would have known that Pharaoh doesn't give free wine to treacherous, fat, good-for-nothing kitchen staff!

Do I sound bitter? That man would have let me die for his crime and not even said anything, if he could have got away with it.

And then we had those dreams. Seriously weird stuff, but forceful. My dream was so vivid, so real. It played on my mind all morning. I knew it must mean something, but a fat lot of good that is if you don't know what. And talking of a fat lot of good, that fat lot of nothing, the baker, had a dream too, and not the same one, and he didn't know what it meant either.

Then along came dependable old Joseph. Only he was more knowing than knowable today. He was on his customary round, making sure everything was in his very meticulous order, when he stopped at us. 'Why the long faces, boys?' he asked. 'Why so glum?' And no sooner had I told him my dream than he broke into the biggest smile I had ever seen in that place. 'Why! It's about you. In the dream you had, about squeezing the grapes from three branches of a vine into Pharaoh's cup, the three branches represent the next three days. In three days you will be chief cupbearer again! You're getting out of here!' He sounded so sure.

And then he said, 'Remember me when you get out. I

was brought here from my own land as a slave, and I have done nothing worthy of being sent to this place.' (Told you – everyone in prison always feels they have been a victim of some kind of injustice.)

And I meant to remember him. I really did. I just forgot.

And then the loafing loaf-smith tried to get in on the act, telling Joseph his dream, but it kind of backfired. Of course, his dream was about breadstuffs and baskets, but Joseph said it wasn't like mine. Sure he was going to be leaving the prison in a few days, only in his case it would be feet first.

And then one day after I had been reinstated came Pharaoh's dream. And that was the wildest of all, full of greedy grain and carnivorous cows. I mean, what was that about? When I heard about Pharaoh's dream it reminded me of Joseph. And when I told Pharaoh the story, he sent for him immediately. And once again Joseph has been right. Even Pharaoh could see that. Promoted him straight away, made him first minister. Imagine that.

You wake up on a day like every other – oh, the monotony of prison life. Slopping out, cold porridge, roll call, and spend the rest of the day watching flies. It's so boring in there that even the flies are climbing the walls.

And all of a sudden, completely out of the blue, you, a prisoner in the city's infamous jail, get made into prime minister. How surreal is that? No more cold porridge, but the biggest banquet you've ever seen. Slaves hanging on your every word. 'More quails' eggs, sir? Would you like wine with that? I can especially recommend the white.' And you end the day in a palatial bedroom, more slaves 'just checking that my lord's bed is soft enough and everything is to his liking'.

What a day that must have been.

6 Benjamin

BACKSTORY

Betraying your brother is a serious sin, and Scripture warns more about unfaithfulness than even faithlessness. So, as the heinous nature of what they had done to Joseph began to dawn on the other brothers, it must have been dreadful, and made worse by the fact that they couldn't undo it. But, in the end, circumstances forced them to face up to what they had done.

MONOLOGUE

I was quite young when we sold Joseph. It all seemed like a bit of a game to me then. Laddish things. Adolescent high jinks. I don't think I really grasped what we were doing.

Lowering him into that well was the funniest thing, or so it seemed back then.

There was a buzz about what we were doing, like it wasn't serious. Everyone was talking at once, fast and loud. All sorts of comments were flying round, all sorts of jokes. We all knew Father would disapprove, but it didn't seem important. Somehow our knowledge of his disapproval just made him seem a little more irrelevant, like there was something potent going on which he would be too old and too staid to understand.

It was as if the mood we were in was some kind of reality that you had to be one of us to identify with, to recognise and appreciate.

We all joked about his coat. Father had given him a very expensive coat, one that used all the colours you can get with cloth. We all took turns wearing it and doing our impressions of Joseph.

'Look, look,' someone said. 'Look, this is how he walks.' **[Puts on a cloak and struts around]** And we roared with laughter. Mind you, we'd all had some wine, so anything would have been funny.

'No, no, give me the cloak a minute! It's more like this.' **[Does an even more exaggerated strut]**

'And look,' said someone else. 'This is how he stands.' Everyone roared again.

'Wait – I've got a good one.' **[Puts on a pompous, inane-sounding voice]** 'I've had a dream. And you were all in it. Only you weren't as good at anything as I was. I was, like, amazing, and you all stood round admiring me. In my first dream you were just, like, bowing and stuff. But in my second dream I was the sun, so you were practically worshipping me. Even Mum, even Dad. It was like all the sunshine was coming out of me. I mean, you couldn't even live without me. How about it? Why don't you all worship me now?'

And we laughed so much that I thought we would explode like old wineskins when you try to reuse them. And the lampoons continued.

'He won't need a light in that well – 'cos he's the sun!'

'What about the rest of us? How will we live if the sun has been stuffed down an old well? We should get a giant sling and catapult him into the air.'

'Now that would kill him!'

And there was momentary hush. Someone had said it. The idea of killing him was suddenly in the air, buzzing between us like flies. Only now it all seemed that it would be part of the joke. Just a bit of a laugh. Truss him up. A couple of us haul him to the top of a high tree. Say something like, 'You're the sun. Shine your way out of this.' And throw him. Or if he's too heavy to lift, we could find some venomous snakes and keep dropping them down his well till he finally shut up.

Reuben wasn't with us at that moment. Perhaps things might have turned out different if he had been, but he wasn't. You can never know what might have been.

Suddenly Judah shouted: 'Look, a caravan!' And he pointed. 'Over there. They must be Ishmaelite traders. This is the route from Gilead to Egypt. They're probably taking all sorts of goods to Egypt. We could sell them something else. A slave! What do you say we bring a little sunshine into their lives?'

And before you knew it, we'd taken their cash and sold them Joseph. I didn't stop to think about what we were doing. I don't think any of us did. We all just supposed that 'cos no one said it was wrong, it must be all right.

I do regret it now. I think I knew it was wrong as soon as Reuben got back. The others were still high on the feeling of what we'd done and didn't really listen to him. But I knew. I knew the look on his face was genuine pain. It seemed to prophesy all the anguish of the years that lay ahead of us. In the end the arguments stopped, and we all returned in silence to Father at Kiriath Arba, each accompanied by the accusations or defences of his own thoughts.

The years passed. I don't so much remember the way

Joseph must have looked when he realised what we were about to do as I recall the look on Reuben's face when he realised what we'd done.

When the famine became so desperate that Father sent my brothers to Egypt, he wouldn't let me go. You see, I am the only living son of his second wife, Rachel. He always regarded her as his first wife, his true love. So when they returned without Simeon, saying the only way the Egyptians would release him was if I accompanied them on another trip, he wouldn't hear of it.

'My son will not go down there with you. His brother is dead, and he is the only one I've got. If anything happens to him it will bring me down to the grave. No – no, no, no! He's not going, and that's final.'

But in the end hunger drove him to agree. And here I am. In Egypt. Simeon has been returned unharmed. And we are waiting for Pharaoh's right-hand man to arrive and tell us why he wanted to see us all. Reuben says we are being punished because of Joseph. He says that we sold Joseph into misery, and that's why this misery has come to us. He says that God is requiring us to give a reckoning for Joseph's blood. He may have a point.

The Most Famous Fight in History –
David and Goliath

Reading 1 Samuel 17:17–29 will give you the background to this story.

7 Eliab

BACKSTORY

As the oldest brother of the man God had chosen to be king, Eliab became consumed by resentment and jealousy. He belittled David and his achievements and also projected his own bad attitudes onto David.

MONOLOGUE

I cannot believe that Father sent him here. Does he think this is a playground for the lad? Doesn't he realise? This is an army camp on the edge of what will shortly be a serious battleground. We come here, risking our lives for our king and our God, and what does Father do? He sends his youngest lad on some trivial errand. I'm sure they both think it's a picnic out here.

'I have brought some bread. . . And some wine. . . Would anyone like a goblet of wine? How about a roll? I've got some cheese, you know. . .'

I'm not saying that Dad meant any harm. I don't actually know what he was thinking. I'm sure he thought that some extra rations would cheer everyone up. And I'm sure he meant for the lad to see some real courage in action. He's been very sheltered. All his working life he's done nothing, really, just lived off the rest of us. Not his fault, of course. Can't blame him; he hasn't really got a trade. Dad's tried with him. Even given him a few sheep to look after. But I don't know. Often happens with the youngest. The dad spoils him and the mum dotes on him and he never really comes to much. Still, we all do our best with him.

Then there's that embarrassing business with Samuel the prophet. If you ask me, I think that the whole thing has got to the dotty old man. I think he's lost it. First his sons go off the rails, which, to be fair, is not his fault. But then he falls out with Saul. Now I know some people think Saul is not the man he was, but it was a very public bust-up, and Samuel became a virtual recluse after that – until one day when he turns up at our place saying he's going to anoint another king.

I thought it all sounded very dubious, and not a little eccentric, but I played along, just to see how it turned out. At one point I actually thought he was going to pick me, being the oldest and quite a lot taller and stockier than the others. But he turned out to be even more off-beam than I had realised, dismissing all six of us. Then there's a long, embarrassed silence, and finally he asks, 'Have you got any more sons?' What sort of a question is that? 'Well,' Dad says, 'only David. But he's just a lad. We let him look after the sheep.' And that was that. Samuel called him, anointed him and then went home. And no one thought any more of it. Not even David mentioned the episode. I mean, I'm sure he knows it was daft. But then he turns up here, shouting his mouth off about things he knows nothing about, and suddenly I'm not so sure.

This evening I saw him wandering around carrying his sling and an empty bag. I asked what he was doing, but he wouldn't tell me. Said something about talking to King Saul. I know he's been asked to sing for the king once or twice, and he's not bad. Actually – that could be something he could do. It's not a trade in the usual sense of the word, but it's something. But I don't think the king is in the mood for taking military advice from a lad who strums the lute, and I have told him not to interfere.

The thing is, he's really still just a boy. I suppose I should look out for him, but when does he ever listen? This whole thing could end in tears. I'm his older brother, and he needs to show a little respect. He's got a lot to learn. If anything happens to him I know Dad's going to lose it with me. But what can I do? He just doesn't listen.

I can't really believe it, but I'm a little concerned that he reckons he's got an idea how we can kill this giant soldier that the Philistines keep trotting out. He doesn't understand strategy, you see. He doesn't realise that there is a military advantage in letting the enemy think they've wrong-footed us. Saul and Abner know exactly what they're doing. I'm sure they don't need advice from a lad with a few sheep, and they won't be impressed if he tries to offer it. Could reflect badly on all of us – I mean the whole family.

Still, I'm sure they won't stand for any of his nonsense.

8 Abner

BACKSTORY

Abner was Saul's cousin, and a mighty warrior. At one time, he was commander-in-chief of Saul's army. He was an ambitious and unscrupulous soldier. Read 1 Samuel 17:55. While Saul and Abner appeared to be ignorant of who David was related to, some scriptures suggest that there was some awareness of his identity. But Saul's mental state was such that he might easily have forgotten David and his occasional serving in the courts as a musician, although Abner's emphatic denial of any knowledge of David's family might be thought by some to be a little over the top.

MONOLOGUE

I have to tell you, I'm troubled. And I'm not often troubled. There's not usually much that can't be sorted out with a hefty sword or an axe. I'm the first one into most fights; it shows the men how it's done. No point in pussyfooting around when a straightforward punch will settle most things – except that this situation is a little different.

To start with, there is a lot at stake. We've assembled a pretty sizable force here, and that's not easy. It takes months to get it right, what with training the farmers to be soldiers, which is not a straightforward job. And it's certainly not cheap.

And now there's a lot of grumbling and murmuring going on. No one has had the front to come to me, of course. But I know it's going on. Saul has lost the confidence of the men, and word is getting out that we've been caught on the hop by this giant Philistine. And the truth is we have. This giant comes along and says that we should put the whole outcome of the war on one fight. No way are we going to do that! The truth is: nor are they. But it has seriously demoralised the men.

Then the king lets it be known that anyone who kills this giant will get riches – and tax breaks – and even his daughter, Merab. But that is going about it all the wrong way. To start with, we haven't said how much money, and no one's going to risk getting their head staved in for a tax break. And Merab – what can I say? None of the lads are exactly falling over themselves to get Merab. I wouldn't say it to Saul's face, but she's not a great looker. All his girls are – to put it mildly – snobs, and anyway no one's quite sure how long Saul's going to last if he carries on like this. All he's done is tell the whole country that we don't know what to do, and that we're desperate. Now, he's my king, and I will fight for him as long he is king. But this whole situation is seriously nuts, and every day we don't do something it gets worse.

However, today one glimmer of hope has appeared. It's not much, but it might be the best we've got. A youth called David, Eliab's kid brother, has come up with some supplies from his old man's farm. And he's got it into his head that he's going to fight this giant. No mistaking that he's a wiry lad and quick on his feet, but he has no experience of battle, and he looked like a turkey in a sack when he tried some armour on!

So why is this a glimmer of hope? Well, for one thing, Eliab hates him. He says he's just worried for his brother, but he's not fooling anyone. All the men know he hates him. He's done nothing but bad-mouth the boy since he got here, and when a runner came saying that David was here with some provisions, Eliab looked like he'd swallowed a live goat.

The point is that when the young man loses – and no one's putting any money on him winning, even though there are some very good odds on offer in the camp – when the young man loses, none of the troops are going to care. I'll say this, though: he can play and sing like he's come straight from the mountain of God. But unless he sings the giant a lullaby and sends him off to sleep, then this youth is history.

But the best thing is, it doesn't really matter if he dies, and we might even manage to turn him into a kind of martyr. Of course, we'll have to withdraw, and that will cost everyone a fortune, but it can all be explained. All we have to say is, 'We had decided to catch the giant off guard – lull him into an arrogant complacency before we struck. But just before we had a chance to launch our surprise attack, this plucky young man came forward, and we couldn't stop him in time. It's tragic. And although no one knew, it turned out that the young man's own brother was on the battle line when it happened. He's devastated. But no one seriously expects that the fact that a lumbering giant killed a brave but inexperienced young man is going to change anything. We are still determined: the war goes on just the same.'

And what if David wins? Well. . . David could win. . . I

suppose. . . anything's possible. . . But if he does, it'll change everything. No one's going to want to follow Saul after that. It may take a little time, but the winds of change will start blowing. Who knows? Maybe Saul will go. And Jonathan's a good leader. With David at his side, I think a change of king could even be in the offing.

9 A youth that met David on the way to the battle

BACKSTORY

The youth himself: 'I can hardly believe it: Dad's going to let me go to where the army is camped. You see, our neighbour, well, she's a widow. Her husband died in an accident. I think he got killed by a neighbour's bull or something. Well, that's what everyone says. Anyway, her only son is camped with the army now, and she wants to send him some food. But she can't really go herself, what with her being a lady and all. So Dad said he'd get me to take it. I've just been to her house to get it. There's not much. Even I eat more than that, and I'm not a soldier! But now I'm really going to the army camp. I can't believe it.'

MONOLOGUE

[At the end of the day following the backstory]

It is still really hot tonight, and so clammy! It's been this way all day. Hope it's going to cool off a little now, as the sky is so clear. There is a really big moon as well.

It is not at all how I imagined it. When I knew I was coming here, to the army of the Lord, right on the battle line, I thought it would be something brave. I imagined the excitement of seeing God's army – all the men across the land gathered to defend their homes and families and proclaim the greatness of God.

I grew up on the story of the Siege of Jabesh Gilead: how the Ammonites laid siege to the city and said they were going to pull one eye out of everyone when they surrendered. I mean, that is really horrible. I'm so glad I wasn't there. Then news about it got to the court of King Saul, and they all began weeping and that. But King Saul heard them, and when he heard the Ammonite threats, the Spirit of God came on him, and he called men from all over in the name of God, and they won. The city was saved, and everyone started to believe and hope again.

On the way here I met this guy – I think he said his name was David. I reckon he was expecting the same as I was, only he looked even more disappointed than I am when we got here. All the way here he was talking about whether there would be a battle while we were here. But he wasn't afraid at all – not that I am either. He just kept saying things like how great it would be if there was a battle after we arrived, and stuff like that. But when that giant started yelling at us, David really changed. I reckon it got to him. He looked really bothered, and then he just went off.

I've wandered around the camp all day looking for him, but he's completely vanished. I've met loads of the men of the army, but really they're just men of the land – farmers, shepherds and such. And I suppose there are a few craftsmen – carpenters, weavers and that. But no one has seen David. Though I don't think most of them would have noticed.

The only thing I noticed is that there weren't any blacksmiths, and there weren't any weapons. I guess that the blacksmiths the Philistines didn't kill were all scared off. Anyway, I think the Philistines robbed all their tools and stuff. The point is, there were hardly any weapons, and none of the men I met were really soldiers. They all seemed miserable, missing their wives and families. And most of them were worried about their farms or their work. There was a lot of complaining, mainly about Saul. Everyone seems fed up. And I haven't seen a single sword all day.

We're never going to win like this. What has happened to us since Gilead? I thought it would be so easy, everyone raring to go. But it's not like that at all.

I've just walked back through the camp. All I can hear is men snoring, tents flapping and mice scuttling around the supplies. No one's praying, and definitely no one's getting ready for a battle. And all 'cos of just one man. I know he's a big man, a giant, but he's still only a man. Someone must say that God can be trusted. And someone must teach these Philistines a lesson, show them that God should be feared. Everyone knows something must happen, but no one knows what.

Just now I thought I saw David wandering along the stream picking up stones, but then when I looked again he was gone. Everyone's asleep. That giant's boast about turning us all into slaves has begun to get to me now. I keep hearing the sound of him laughing and yelling 'cowards, fools', stuff like that. Now it's got dark, it's really beginning to get to me. I think I might go home. I mean, I've delivered the food. I don't really need to be here. But I'm going to try to find David first. Then we can go back together. I am sure that was him that I saw further along the hill. I reckon he might be thinking of going home, too. I wonder what he wanted with those stones. . .

The Judgement of Solomon

Reading 1 Kings 3:16–28 will give you some background to the story. Solomon realised at the outset of his reign that he would need wisdom to lead the people of God. His prayer was: 'Give your servant a discerning heart to govern your people and to distinguish between right and wrong. For who is able to govern this great people of yours?' (1 Kings 3:9).

10 A servant woman from the court

BACKSTORY

This painful incident helped to cement Solomon's reputation for wisdom.

MONOLOGUE

I remember the day. Word had got out that the king was sitting in state at the palace in Jerusalem. This would usually be the cue for dignitaries, minor officials and businessmen of significance to come to see him. The day would then be taken up with various affairs of state. It was our job to entertain these bigwigs. They had to have plenty of food and drink and be made comfortable and put at their ease.

It can be a tall order. It takes a certain type of person and a certain way of behaving. You're more than a household servant. You're a servant at court, a role that carries import and dignity and, yes, status – all of which you need in abundance to do this job.

Which made this particular day all the more unusual. We prepared as normal – organising the furnishings, the fittings, the kitchen servants, a musician. So much to be in place before the doors even open! But when we go to greet the guests, the first in are two prostitutes. Not at all what we expected, and my superior was about to tell them to leave when King Solomon came striding into the hall and spoke to them. 'Ladies!' First time anyone has called them that, I'll be bound. 'Ladies, if you would be so kind as to wait here, I will commence court in half an hour.' And he strode through the hall to the royal reception.

He must have known what they were, so we set about making them welcome.

They both looked dreadful. Given that their profession requires them to publicly look their best while privately exacting its own unique toll, they still looked dreadful. And when I heard their story, I understood why.

Each had had a child, and one had died, but now they were both contesting whose child it was that had died.

Each sounded believable.

I spoke to the first woman, and she was the more tearful of the two. The way she described the living child, which she was adamant was hers, she made him sound adorable – constantly laughing and giggling, full of hugs and cuddles, and with that unique personality that every mother adores in her own son. You had to believe she was describing her own child, but which child? Was this the pained recollection of a mother who couldn't accept what had occurred? Her tone sounded as though she believed she had right on her side, but that alone didn't mean she had.

The second woman had greater confidence. She was less apologetic, more matter of fact, and seemed far more sure of herself. She spoke of how a great wrong had been done. She really made you feel the shock of waking to hear the other woman wailing when she realised her baby was dead. She described the spreading horror that came over her as that woman's grief turned to wild accusation, and she realised that she would be neither comforted nor dissuaded from this delusion. Needless to say, it was not her initiative to bring all this to the king.

Trouble is, I believed them both. But one of them was lying. Whether from grief or from callous manipulation, I couldn't tell.

It sounds obvious to say that God knew.

He watched over the final earthly moments of the child who died. He held his spirit in his arms and welcomed him to his courts.

I was in court when King David was on the throne. I was just a young girl when Bathsheba's first child sickened and died. I remember watching over the king as he lay prostrate for days in the palace, praying and pleading for the life of his child. But nothing throughout my life has ever had such a profound effect on me as the day the child died. King David showed such dignity and faith that day.

When the king heard his child was dead, he got up from the ground and washed, changed his clothes and put on lotions. Then he went to the Temple to worship, before coming home and having us prepare him some food. We asked him about this, and I'll never forget his reply: 'I will go to him, but he will not return to me.' Such gravity, such assurance.

The departed child is in heaven's palace. I know that. Such is the peace and tranquillity above. It's down here that we need someone to bring us calm and wisdom.

And I wondered what King Solomon could do.

When he heard the story, everyone was silent, waiting on his judgement with baited breath.

It seemed like an age till he spoke, and when he did I was shocked. He had earlier shown such kindness and gentleness listening to their words. But now, all that patience seemed to have vanished, evaporated as though it were a mirage.

'Is the living child here? Good. Kill him, chop him up and give half to each mother.'

His words were greeted with a gasp from the court and a shriek of 'No!' from the first woman and a hollow laugh from the other, who called across the court to the first, 'Neither of us gets him. At least that's fair.'

There was another moment's silence, and then the king spoke again. 'Give the child to the woman who cried "no". She is his mother.'

As soon as he spoke, all of us understood. If we do right, in the end God will see to it that we come out right.

11 The mother

BACKSTORY

Listen to the words of James in *The Message*: 'Do you want to be counted wise, to build a reputation for wisdom? Here's what you do: live well, live wisely, live humbly. It's the way you live, not the way you talk, that counts. . . Real wisdom, God's wisdom, begins with a holy life. . .' (James 3:13–17). Solomon pointed both women to such wisdom that day.

MONOLOGUE

Imagine. Me at court. Actually meeting the king, and him listening to me!

If I hadn't been there because I wanted to get my son back, it might even have been fun. As it was, it was the most terrifying thing I have ever done.

But I knew I had to. I just had to. Joel means everything to me. My own childhood wasn't that great, and I wanted him at least to be with someone who loved him.

Sometimes I hear people talking about happy memories from their childhood, playing with other children in the street, sitting listening to someone's granny telling stories, even the fun of family meals. I used to long for memories like that. I even invented some for myself, comforting fictions to tell myself, pretending that I used to have a life.

We were always a poor home. I can't really recall life before Dad died, but Mum said that she and Dad were happy. I don't remember. But after he died, we all had to move in with Dad's brother's family. And that made for an unhappy home. My aunt didn't like Mum and resented us kids.

Oh, I know Mum wanted me and my brother, but I don't think anyone else ever wanted me. I was always going to be poor, and no one would marry me. That's what my aunt would tell me. Constantly. And so that's what I thought.

It never seemed such a big step. When you're not wanted and think you have no future, becoming a woman on the streets doesn't seem like such a big step.

I should have known that I would get pregnant. The other girls used to see it as an occupational hazard. And so the story comes full circle. An unwanted mum has an unwanted kid. And round we go again.

Only I didn't want that. Just before Joel was born I remember thinking how I wanted that little bundle in my arms instead of in my middle. He wasn't going to be unwanted.

I had chosen my way of life, or at least it seemed to have chosen me. But I didn't want to raise him as a nuisance that gets in the way of my rather miserable existence.

I know it sounds odd, but he made me happy. For the first time in my life I had someone other than myself. I know that my life has been anything but charmed, and if I'm honest, I've made some pretty poor choices. Even now I still make bad choices and even worse mistakes, but I wanted this to turn out different.

From the moment he was born, Joel was always chortling and giggling. And he has always been heaven to hold. Just looking at his tiny face used to make my insides go kind of crinkly. Bathing him. Feeding him. Brushing his hair. Playing with him and his rattle. The man over the road made that for him.

It kind of let me touch another world. A kind world. A clean world. A world where you can love and be loved instead of lusted after.

I began to think that this life could be more than the dirt and the mess that had been crammed into my bit of existence. And then, one morning, I woke up and there beside me was this child, cold and motionless. Only it wasn't Joel. Where was Joel?

I had moved in with Nediva when Joel was born. She was one of the girls, and we thought we would be company for each other. We were both first-time mums, and though we're very different people, neither of us had family that still wanted to know us. It might have worked. I don't know.

But then Nediva's baby died. And she took mine. That's fact. It's vicious and callous and desperate, but that's what happened.

I think she just didn't know what to do. I know I couldn't live without Joel. But I would have had to if she had had had her way.

That's why I went to the king. That's a laugh – a common prostitute thinking that the king will see her!

The other girls said I was mad. I think most of them believed me, even though I don't think any of them were quite sure. But they were sure I was mad. I don't think they were wrong, but sometimes you've just got to do whatever it takes.

And that's what's made me think. You know the king said to chop Joel in two? I couldn't have let him do that. I know now that it was a test, but I didn't know that when he said it.

All of a sudden, I realised that there are some things that I won't do, and other things that are better than giving up on life, even if they're hard. I would have given Joel to Nediva, but I would never have let him die. I made a good choice, a right choice, a choice for someone besides myself.

Solomon gave me back Joel. But he also gave me back me. And I'm not going to waste either of us.

The First Healing of a Leper

The complete story of Naaman is to be found in 2 Kings 5. Naaman was from Aram, and thus not one of the people of God. He was commander of the army of the king of Aram, and he was also a leper. In those days leprosy was incurable. It slowly destroyed the bodies of its victims and would ultimately prove fatal. It usually began with a speck on the skin and gradually spread over the body. However, the Hebrew word that is translated 'leprosy' covered many different skin conditions. (Leviticus 13 shows that not all of these were contagious.)

12 Naaman's wife

BACKSTORY

Naaman's wife recognised the good, kind and honest heart of her young Israelite slave girl. She had been taken captive by raiders, ripped away from her home and family, made a slave in a foreign country and bought by Naaman. Despite this, she still loved Naaman and his wife and was concerned about his condition.

MONOLOGUE

I bought the child Shira from the market as a serf, to do some of the chores around the house and the kitchen gardens. She is still young and has a lot to learn, but she appeared to have accepted her lot when I bought her and is not proving too hard to train. Of course, the young ones are easier to mould, although at the same time they are often clumsier.

This one was an Israelite, taken by a raiding party last summer, but she was from a very poor family and is actually better off with us. At least, that's what I think.

Anyhow, she is self-assured and sparky, and sings constantly and talks all the time about her village and her tribe, but without being tiresome. The other day, she told me a story that may hold out some real hope for Naaman. It's not been easy for him these past two years.

She talks of a mystic called Eli Sha or some such. Apparently, he can feed the starving and even give life to the dead. With that kind of power, you would think he would be king, but apparently he lives in obscurity, appearing when it suits him, doing some miracle and then disappearing. He has an extraordinary reputation in her land, despite his opposition to the gods of the land.

Life has been hard these past two years for Naaman. Everyone knows it. He's risen through the ranks to the very top – chief army commander of the troops of the king of Aram. And highly respected. Even the king says, 'Naaman's my secret weapon. Never lost a battle under his command. Never. Brave as a lion. You should hear some of the stories they tell about him in the ranks!'

And then he starts on the stories. Not suitable for a refined audience's ears. Too much blood. Not all the stories are even suitable for his wife's ears, but I don't give those ones too much credence. I mean, they are told by some very rough men.

Anyhow, he's right at the top of his career when his skin gets covered in this white, blotchy stuff. The medics say it's not contagious. Better not be, or the king will have to ditch him. Come to that, I would ditch him. I love him, of course, but I'm no heroine – no long-suffering angel – and I certainly don't want to die. It used to be a thrill to be seen with him, but now that's gone.

I don't particularly like personal contact in the light. And he wears a long-sleeved robe whenever he appears in public. We had it made by the country's finest seamstress. It makes him look rather dashing, but you know what people are thinking. He says he doesn't care what people think as long as the troops follow him into battle, which they always

do. The men are loyal, more so these days than ever. They
see him more as a father than just their commanding
officer. Their wives are another story – lowered tones when
the officers' wives meet! Pitying looks, though no one
would dare give those looks a voice.

He says he doesn't care, but I know he misses the adula-
tion from the crowds and just being able to be part of normal life, like we used to.

So I listened more carefully when Shira started on about
this Eli Sha. She told me all his stories, and then she said, 'If
only my master would see this prophet from my country. . .
He would cure him.' Well, you wonder if she's just an
impressionable youth with multi-coloured memories from
her homeland, but once she had said it, she just kept on
about it. In the end I told Naaman.

I don't know what I expected him to say. Naaman's
always been kind of . . . kind of devout, I suppose. Not
superstitious, not even what you might call religious, but
spiritual.

This Eli Sha sounds a fiery man. Had blazing rows at court.
Told the king that he held him beneath contempt. Sounds a
bit like my Naaman – never one to keep his mouth shut.

Seems he has a thing about his God. Says his is the only
God – a view not shared by his king. Gets him almost poetic,
and he is always quoting the sacred writings of his people.
Shira has learnt loads of it by heart.

One bit goes, 'What God is asking you today is not too
difficult for you or beyond your reach. Not up in heaven,
nor beyond the sea. No, the word is very near you.'

Now, Naaman likes that kind of poetry, although I've
never known him to try something unless everyone else
said it was too difficult.

I thought I would tell him some of Shira's stories and see what he thought. When I did, he thought for a while, and then he said, 'This is good. A long journey to make, a mysterious prophet to find, a challenge to confront. I will go.'

Told you. I've never known him to try something unless everyone else said it was too difficult.

13 Naaman's companion

BACKSTORY

A soldier: 'The army has always been noted for its bravery in battle and loyalty to Naaman, our commanding officer. That trust between him and his troops was established when Naaman was a young general. He never chose the safety of the rear of the battle. He always led from the front and fought shoulder to shoulder with the men. From the beginning, his men would have done just about anything for their leader. But none of us could combat his illness.'

MONOLOGUE

This is going to take a lot of explaining when we get home. Not that anyone will be other than over the moon. Naaman has always been popular, and I think his illness only made him more so.

Made him a little more human, a little more approachable. After a while, that is. Of course, he retained his ability to curse and call down the wrath of the gods when the situation called for it. But at other times he seemed to have found more patience and understanding than I remember from the old Naaman, the one before he got the disease.

At first, like when he first got it, he was unendurable. An hour with him was like a day trip through hell. The medics had just told him that they couldn't fix it and that it wouldn't ever go away. Talk about a bear with a sore head! He used every swear word, insult, obscenity and blasphemy that I've ever known, quite a few I didn't know, and a number that no one knew but you could guess what they meant by the wild eyes and the wrath in his voice. Once, he actually showed us what he meant by using a kitchen slave as target practice. I won't tell you what he was throwing at him.

Over the months his temper reduced to merely volcanic magnitude, and in time it subsided to a point where he could go for days without destroying anything that crossed his path. Finally, as I said before, he became more. . . Well, more. . . Well, less harsh and more reachable.

But in all this time he still ran a tight operation when it came to anything military. He was never less than the best in the field, and we all knew it. Our experience of him has never been less than professional, if a little stressful.

But this last trip has caught us all by surprise. Going over to Israel is something that is usually done by gangs of marauders, not seasoned military commanders. It was all a bit surreal at first. As I recall, it went something like this.

Naaman's wife gets an Israelite slave. So far, so good. The slave knows a mystic with miraculous powers. Now it begins to get kooky. The slave dares to tell Naaman's wife to get Naaman to go and see him. Naaman's wife tells Naaman. Still with me? It gets richer. Naaman believes what the slave girl has said. And here's where it passes beyond anything I've ever known. Naaman tells the king. The king believes it and arranges an official diplomatic trip to the region. By now, there's hardly anyone else still keeping up with the story who thought what we were about to do was even slightly sane, and absolutely no one left who thought it was normal.

But still we went. Well, the king had ordered it. No one's about to question the king.

Would you believe me if I told you that this mystic didn't even bother to greet Naaman? Didn't even come out of his house. Just sent a servant out to tell Naaman to go. Said he should wash in the nearest river.

Naaman was incandescent.

'I thought that at least he would come out and see me – stand and call on the name of his God, wave his hand and cure me of my leprosy!

'Aren't Abana and Pharpar in Damascus better rivers than any stagnant backwater that I can find here in Israel? Couldn't I wash in them and be healed?'

It was like the day the medics told him about his illness, complete with ranting, cursing and throwing things. 'Pack up,' he said. 'We're heading back.'

Now, I'm not usually one to question orders, but this one struck me as insane, so I told him. 'Father, if the prophet had told you to do some great thing, you would have done it. So why not try this? There's only a few of us here, and we've come a long way for this.'

And, amazingly, he listened. It took him a while on his own not saying anything, but he listened.

If I'm honest, I was amazed. I would have bet all I've got on him not listening.

Something happened when he went off on his own.

Now he's been to the river (and he was right, it was a bit of a backwater – I thought he would change his mind when we all saw it), but now that he's been there, and washed and been healed, well, I'm not sure I know what to make of it.

But I know what *he* made of it.

We were all for heading back the moment he came from the river. There were a few amazed words from all of us, a few wild whoops and some fairly wild tackles as we all clapped each other on the back. In fact, there was more celebration between the few of us there on that riverbank than when we were with the army last time we wiped the floor with the enemy. But none of us thought about going back to find the mystic.

None of us except Naaman, that is.

The end of this whole bizarre incident has changed him even more than when it began.

I suppose it was only natural, and certainly no more than the king would have expected for our national pride, to shower a few gifts on the mystic.

Except he wouldn't take any.

And that could have been it. The end. Naaman goes home and everyone is happy. Only there is an intriguing little footnote.

When the mystic declined any gifts, Naaman asked for as much earth as a pair of mules can carry, saying that he was never again going to make burnt offerings to any other god than the God of this mystic.

Somehow I think more washed into him than off of him that day.

14 Naaman

BACKSTORY

Naaman's condition must have been a concern and frustration to him. As a military strategist, he was used to planning and fighting his way out of anything. A human enemy he could face fearlessly in battle, but this disease was a different kind of enemy, one with which he could not contend.

MONOLOGUE

I'm just a man. Some have said I am a lucky man. Some have called me fearless. Most have said I wouldn't suffer fools gladly. And some have called me insufferably arrogant. And I guess all of them are right. But in reality, I'm just a man.

A man who met his God on a lonely little riverbank.

I didn't go expecting much. I just couldn't shake the feeling that I had to go. Everything in me told me not to go, told me that this Eli Sha was a sham, a fraudster who didn't even dare see me.

But I went. And standing there on that riverbank I was suddenly overcome.

Overcome by the realisation of how small I was, the realisation that this all mattered so little.

The world has known greater generals than I. There have been more courageous heroes, more passionate poets and lovers, more careful thinkers.

For a moment all I could think of was little Shira, my wife's kitchen slave. She's really only a child, but she had something that I didn't. Me, the mighty Naaman. Her, the kitchen slave. How can she have anything at all? How can she have more than me?

But standing there on that riverbank I suddenly knew that she did. It wasn't about *things*. Not about position. Not about reputation. What little she had of all that, she lost when the raiders took her from her home.

But she had a life that I lacked.

The misfortune of that raid hadn't taken from her what the misfortune of my illness had taken from me.

I can be determined, resolute. I have never conceded defeat in my entire life. I've never conceded anything, never surrendered. But what I had left was steely determination. Something had drained from me. I didn't notice it going, but I knew then that it had gone.

I was consumed by a longing for her innocence, her simplicity, her faith.

Yes, that was it! I wanted her trust in her God. Something in me ached for even a minute of knowing her God like she used to say she knew him, and my life fell away from me. I'm glad no one was near me then, because I wept.

I could recall my confident assertions about life, but they all seemed so hollow. And in that moment I first spoke to her God.

It wasn't a great prayer – more of a stuttering apology – but he heard it.

[Drops to his knees and raises his hands to show that he is reiterating his earlier prayer]

'I've never surrendered. Never needed to. But I think I need to now.

[Takes a deep breath]

I surrender. I surrender my entire life to you. All my outward success. All my inner emptiness. Everything.

'If you ask it, I will stay a leper. I want nothing as much as I want you. I don't even want to leave this river without you.

'You are bigger than I am, and I yield in the face of my own insignificance. If a little slave girl can have more than me by knowing you. . .

'I want to know you. I want that more than I have ever wanted anything in my life.

'In a moment I'm going into this fairly muddy river.

'The man said that I will be healed. I'm still not sure about that. But if I meet you, it is enough.'

[He stands up]

So, by now you've probably heard most of the rest, and you can see I've never looked healthier.

You may not have heard what Eli Sha said to me afterwards.

I returned to his house. This time he took me in. The smile we exchanged was enough.

Enough for him to know I had met his God, and enough for me to know he knew it.

I asked him the one thing that had troubled me since that experience on the river bank.

'I am a servant and close companion of the king of Aram. He will expect me to go to the temple of Rimmon with him as soon as I return. And when he enters the temple to bow down to his god, he always leans on my arm, and so I have to bow too. When I bow down in the temple of Rimmon, may the Lord forgive me for this.'

Another smile, and he said, 'I can't tell you what to do. Go in peace and remain in peace. God's peace will keep you.'

It would be so much easier if there was just a set of rules, like being a soldier. But it seems there isn't.

I suppose with a new faith and a new life comes a new way to live it. Maybe I have become like Shira – a child having to learn about life all over again.

Famine – Account of a Miracle

Jehoram was the son of Ahab and Jezebel. He was king of the northern kingdom of Israel. (Confusingly, there was another man named Jehoram, who became king of the southern kingdom of Judah.) In 2 Kings 3 it says he did evil in the eyes of God, but not as much as his father and mother. Israel was often invaded by Syria, despite receiving warnings from the prophet Elisha calling them to repent of idolatry. Out of his kindness, God often did extraordinary miracles, giving military victory to this recalcitrant nation. This is an account of one such miracle. Reading 2 Kings 7 will give you the background to these stories.

15 An officer in the court of King Jehoram

BACKSTORY

A fellow officer: 'I think we should be careful not to under-estimate Elisha. I know most of my comrades think that he's a charlatan, but I'm not so certain. I was there the day he gave us the strategy that defeated Moab. True, he was very rude to the king. As I recall, he said something like, "What have we got in common? Go to the false prophets of your parents. If King Jehoshaphat wasn't here, I wouldn't even notice you." But then he told us how to win the bat-tle. He could be about to do something similar with the Arameans. And whatever he says about King Jehoram, it's victories like the one over Moab that we really need. Every-one loves a winner.'

MONOLOGUE

It isn't easy being an army officer when your city is under siege. It's even harder if you live in the palace. People so easily misunderstand. We do share in the privations of the ordinary people. But we also need to keep order and discip-line. It is only to the enemy's advantage if the city disinte-grates into chaos.

And we need to ensure that food and drink are properly rationed. That's why people have to pay for these things even when the need is desperate – especially when the need is desperate. Although this is done with the best of intentions, we understand that all this is, to say the least, tiresome, especially if you are poor. The poor, of all people, naturally resent these troubles, trials and tribulations, and they vent a good deal of their resentment on those of us charged with distributing any food. Not that everyone is grateful for what we distribute. We usually get all of their abuse and frustration taken out on us. For my part, I would rather be in my chariot in the thick of battle than end up policing this rabble.

The other day, a common woman accosted King Jehoram with some story about her having killed, cooked and eaten her own son, and far from being ashamed she was demanding that the king help her kill another kid to eat him as well. That really upset the king, and I mean *really* upset him.

Worst of all is that so-called prophet Elisha. He claims that all this is the king's fault. He preaches publicly that the king has done evil in the eyes of God. He has hardly ever met him! Last time they did meet, Elisha refused to even look at or acknowledge the king. I don't understand why the king tolerated him for so long.

But it looks as though this time his patience is exhausted. As soon as he had got rid of that woman, he spoke to me privately: 'Kill Elisha. Cut off his head.'

Well, you can't get clearer than that. But we should have foreseen that Elisha would do something outrageous out of the blue. If I didn't know better, I'd swear he even hears our private conversations. He just turns up this morning, bold as brass, and announces to the crowd, 'It'll all be over by this time tomorrow. The siege will be ended. The famine will be ended. You will be buying flour and barley in the market.'

At that, someone called out, 'How much?' And, cool as anything, Elisha replied as though he had it with him, and he was just an ordinary market trader: 'Fifteen litres of flour for only two pieces of silver. But wait! There's more. Fifteen litres of barley for only one piece of silver.'

The crowds cheered. Simpletons. How anyone can fall for such unashamed posturing I will never understand. I called out to him, 'Look, last week you couldn't even get half a bag of plant seeds for that. Oh, you could buy the head of a scrawny old donkey, but it cost fifty times that. Don't be deceived by this old fool. Even if God opens the floodgates of heaven, this couldn't happen.'

He replied, 'You will see it with your own eyes, but you won't eat any of it.' And again the crowd cheered. They are such sheep, so easily swayed. Let's see who they believe tomorrow, when they still have no food, and later, when Elisha's severed head is found in the street.

16 A leper

BACKSTORY

In biblical times, lepers were outcasts, excluded from the community and any semblance of normality, living on the very margins of society. The fact that God chose to work through these four shows his desire to work with those we might pass by.

MONOLOGUE

I never asked for this. I never asked for none of it. I never asked the priest to come round. Oh no. That was them busybodies in the neighbourhood. 'Isaac,' they says. 'Isaac! I reckon you should get that arm looked at.'

Where's the harm? A longer sleeve on my tunic and they'd never have known. A little spot, that's all it was. It's not even my whole arm even now, and that's ten years. Ten years! I mean, where's the sense in ruining a man's life over a little spot? And that's all it was. A little spot.

They says, 'I reckon you should get that arm looked at.' But what they meant was, 'We're going to tell the priest. We don't want anything here that could be catching.'

And that was it. No ifs. No buts. No mercy. And no choice. It's out you go. No question.

I don't think it is leprosy. It hasn't got much bigger in the last five years. And I'm stuck out of the city like I'm just a shadow, living with all the other shadows. Well, you do – band together, I mean. Some of them might have leprosy – real leprosy, I mean. Not like what I've got. And some of them might be selfish, miserable, devious cretins. But you find a few who are half-way decent and stick with them. There are four of us who stick together.

Even when the siege started we figured we'd all do better pooling what we had. Until it became a case of pooling what we didn't have.

I've heard some dreadful stories about the siege. People get desperate. Little children gnawing dead rats. Or live rats gnawing little babies. Famine's a great leveller. Rich young men, poor old women, some shadowy old lepers. We're all the same. If we don't eat, we die.

Well, as it happens, Abe had this idea. He's never been the sharpest arrow in the quiver, has our Abe.

He wakes up one morning and says, 'I've been thinking.' Well, personally I doubt that, but we all hear him out. I mean, what else are we going to do?

'I've been thinking,' he says. 'We could stay here, outside the city, but there's nothing to eat and soon we'll be dead. We could do that.

'Or, and I've thought a lot about this, we could go inside the city. Officially, we can't do that, 'cos we're lepers. But right now people have more important things to worry about, like there being no food. So we could go into the city, you see. Only thing with that is that there's no food inside the city (as I just said) and we will still wind up dead, only this time inside the city.

'Or. . . we could fool everyone by surrendering to the

Arameans. I mean, it's not like we're going to win, anyway. There's only four of us. So where's the harm? That way we'd be prisoners, see? And what happens to prisoners?

'Well, yes, sometimes they do get killed, so we'd still be dead, only this time it wouldn't be outside the city or inside the city. No, it would be in the Aramean camp. But we couldn't be more dead than if we stayed here.

'But sometimes prisoners get fed. And if we got fed – well, then, we wouldn't be dead. Do you see?'

Now, I'm not one to turn my nose up at an idea, even a stupid idea, if it's the only one we've got. So we went.

Now, this next bit doesn't seem too likely. Abe kept saying, 'Pinch me! I'm dreaming.' I tried explaining to him that that wouldn't work, 'cos it would only mean that he had dreamt someone pinched him.

I know what he meant, though. The Aramean camp was completely deserted. They'd all run away. And it looked like they'd left in a hurry and all. They'd left armour, weapons, clothes, tents, horses, money. They must have been given an almighty scare. They'd left everything – even food in the middle of cooking.

Food. In all our bewilderment and surprise we'd forgotten to be hungry. And here we were, surrounded by the most amazing selection of food. We ate loads. Even Abe, who by now had decided that he couldn't be dreaming 'cos he kept having to swish flies off the food. 'And no one would dream up a fly, would they?'

Abe, whose enthusiasm is matched only by his inability to grasp even the blindingly obvious, was convinced that *we* must have done it – scared them all off. Even wanted to go looking around – see if we could find any men and capture them. 'That would be a turn-up for the books, if we went back to the city with the whole lot of 'em our prisoners. We might even be allowed to stay,' he mused.

Later, after he had wasted a few hours looking for Arameans so they could surrender to him, time which we thought better used by eating and trying on shoes till we found ones that fit, he came back and announced, 'You know what? We've forgotten all the folks at home. They're our brothers and sisters, and they're starving too. It's not right.'

I tried pointing out that they hadn't seemed too bothered when *we* were the ones left out in the cold, but once he finally gets an idea into that head there's no stopping him. So back we went, although not before we had all taken some extra food and money.

At first they didn't believe us. Then they thought we must have been hoodwinked. 'Look,' I said, 'I know my friend seems stupid, but he's dogged. If they had been out there, he would have found them.' In the end they accepted it – after they had sent an advance party, just to make sure.

And what happened next? The first ones to arrive only grabbed all the food, went back to the city and sold it! You could buy a 15-litre bag of flour for two pieces of silver, or you could buy barley for half that. I know that's cheap, especially when there was a famine only yesterday, but considering that we were the ones who found it all, I still think they should have given that money to us.

17 A woman in the crowd

It is possible to be a witness to something, even something with national and spiritual significance, and not be aware of exactly what you witnessed (see John 12:28–30 for an example of this).

MONOLOGUE

Yes, I was there. I was even near enough to hear what they both said. It just sounded like two men having a squabble to me.

Well, now I can see that it was more than that. I mean, I'm not stupid, am I?

It isn't that easy to predict the exact price of anything in the market, even in a normal week. But to be able to predict a sudden, miraculous supply of food and know what it will cost in the market . . . now that's startling. I have to admit to a certain amount of pessimism when I heard what that prophet said, although I wasn't cynical like that army bloke. I just couldn't see how it was going to happen.

I think God understands. At least I hope he does. It's hard to be optimistic when you're starving. It's hard when you have had to watch the old couple across the street starve to death to know what to think, even less how to feel, when a man prophesies that food will be in abundance by tomorrow. I know what old Joe would have said: 'Good luck to him and better luck to us.' He always used to say that about everything. But he isn't here any more, is he?

And that's the point. I mean, we have seen horrors here that no one should ever see. I have heard about things which should never have happened. People eating refuse. Mothers starving themselves so they could give each of their kids a single mouthful. There's even a story going round of a mother who couldn't feed her kid, so she killed him. That would be sickening enough, but there's one version that says she and a neighbour were so hungry that they cooked the body. It's hard to stay in faith against a backdrop like that.

And that prophet wasn't exactly inspiring. It would have been easier to believe if he had been a young, rugged type with fire in his eyes and a voice like thunder. But he looked so run of the mill. You wouldn't expect God to say something so remarkable through someone so unremarkable.

They say that when Moses came from receiving instruction from God his face shone so bright that he had to wear a veil over it. Something like that would have helped me believe that he had heard his news from God. I know this siege has taken it out of us all, but this prophet was so ordinary, and so unkempt.

And then there was what that military man said. Actually, the prophet would have been easier to believe if he had looked more like him. He was an imposing man, a man who sounded accustomed to giving orders. He seemed so incredulous of what the prophet said that he made it sound rather silly.

And yet something in you warmed to what the prophet said. It wasn't just that you were desperate to believe that something like that could happen. In an odd kind of way, it may even have been his ordinariness. You felt he was the same as you. That officer certainly cut a more dashing figure, but he didn't look as if he understood me. To start with it was the way he looked; they must be getting better fed in the palace than everyone else. And that prophet sounded more like my dad used to sound when I was a kid and came running up to him with a cut knee or some tale of unfairness about what my sister had done. He couldn't always stop the bleeding, and he didn't always agree with me about my sister, but there was nothing in the whole world as reassuring as the sound of my father's voice when he said, 'It's OK now.'

Yes, that's it – that's why I warmed to him. He made me feel understood. He made me feel that I could trust him. What he said may have sounded implausible, but somehow I just warmed to him as he spoke. And when I heard the furore this morning, I just knew it must have happened like he said it would.

By the time I got to the market there was a virtual stampede. It was so overwhelming it was dangerous. In fact, I saw them taking a body out from the middle of the crowd.

You know what? It looked a bit like that army officer. Now that would be a turn-up for the books, wouldn't it?

A Time Such as This – Witnesses to the Story of Esther

From the fourth century before Christ comes a tale of intrigue, attempted genocide, and a brave and faithful lady. It happened when the people of God were exiled far from the Promised Land. Reading the book of Esther will give you a good background to these monologues.

18 Memucan

BACKSTORY

The Persian king Xerxes began his reign about 100 years after the Jews were taken into captivity in Babylon and therefore 50 years after his father, King Cyrus (who had since conquered the Babylonians), issued the declaration permitting the Jews to return to their land. So these events occurred among those Jews who chose to remain in foreign lands. The book of Esther tells of a crisis in the history of God's people. A decree was made by Xerxes, at the instigation of one of his officials, that every Jew in his kingdom should be put to death on a certain day. Read Esther 1:10–21, which gives the immediate background to this monologue.

MONOLOGUE

There are times when being in Xerxes' inner circle isn't all it's cracked up to be.

Oh, most of the time it has its benefits. The house is brilliant. You're never short of cash. Everyone respects you. And you get to pick from some of the best slaves for your harem. All in all, this job has its perks.

But you work for it. Xerxes is no slouch. He's got a mind

as sharp as a razor, and he seems to hold every matter of the empire in his brain. And it's no small thing, either, to hold together an empire. You have to depend on your advisors for wisdom, your generals for muscle and your queen for all the lesser matters that smooth the running of the state.

Actually, even the work is a privilege. There's nothing gives you a buzz so much as making successful rulings on major matters of state. It isn't just the power, it's the satisfaction of pulling things round, dispatching the right envoys when they're needed, recognising when military action is called for. But the last few years have been something of a nightmare.

It all started when Queen Vashti refused a summons to come to King Xerxes. To this day I have no idea what she was thinking.

It was about the third year of Xerxes' reign. He had just given a banquet. Everyone who's anyone was there. There were military leaders from right across Persia and Media. There were princes and nobles from all of the provinces. And every possible senior official and advisor. And to cap it all, at the end of the feast, the last seven days, the entire population of Susa was invited.

It was so funny to watch the minor officials trying to make sure that everyone knew who they were, and to see the people who thought they were important sitting where they thought important people should sit and the people who knew they were important sitting anywhere they chose.

But there was one up-and-coming official who gave me the creeps. Haman was his name. You know the sort. The kind of man for whom it isn't enough just to make sure he always wins, but who has to make sure that everyone else loses and the whole world knows about it. As it turned out, he was to play a lead role in the biggest crisis we have ever seen.

For now, though, we had to advise Xerxes about Vashti. No two ways, she had to go. It seems to me that it could set a very dangerous precedent, undermine the role of men in our society. She'd always had such a pejorative way of expressing her point of view. She couldn't say, 'I appreciate the way you are so open in your admiration of me.' No, it was always, 'I suppose you are going to be leering at me all night and trying to get your friends to lust after me.' Actually, I think that was how she ended the row on the night before the incident. The next day we had the refusal. What did she think would happen next? She had to go.

But finding a new queen was not going to be easy. First thing everyone looks at is, well. . . looks. And let's face it, the only thing that most citizens are ever going to know about their queen is what she looks like. So it's important.

But there is so much more to the role than that. The queen has to be an organiser, a socialiser, a keen observer of all those around her. She should be pretty, but she should also be witty, and to a certain extent she should be gritty. Tough enough to take the hard decisions without flinching. And most of all she should be loyal, dutiful, respectful and devoted. Quite a tall order, and Xerxes wanted us to see hundreds of women to help him find the right one. Having to spend over a year of your life looking at hundreds of gorgeous women and seeing which of them had brains and manners to go with their looks was a tough job. But I suppose someone had to do it. . .

The girl we found in the end was a bit of a surprise. I'd expected her to be a daughter of one of the princes. Or at least of one of the nobles. But no one really knew where she came from. There was a rumour that she was related to someone at court and another rumour that she was the great granddaughter of one of Babylon's captives. No one really knew.

But she proved to be an excellent choice. She was everything that Vashti wasn't – charming, urbane, compassionate, cool-headed and, as things turned out, very brave.

I don't think Haman can have known that she was Jewish. I don't think he was interested in knowing things like that. He certainly didn't know that she was descended from the captives who came from Jerusalem, a city far to the west. Nor would he have done what he did to Mordecai and his people had he known that he was related to the queen. He wasn't that stupid. Neither was he so short of enemies that he would deliberately pick a fight with someone who was quite so well connected. I suppose he could still have arranged for him to be mugged and killed one night, but that wasn't really Haman's style. Like I said, when he did something, anything at all, he wanted the reverberations to be felt all round the world and everyone to be in awe of him. This time he got it wrong, and there won't be a next time.

But in everything that has just occurred, I never saw the queen lose her composure. Not once. I guess she must have had her moments, but they must have been private ones. I certainly never noticed.

19 Mordecai

BACKSTORY

Mordecai was familiar with the life and manners of a courtier. He was one of God's people, but also part of life at the Persian court. He moved in circles that made him and his social group wealthy and powerful. He had once saved Xerxes from a plot on his life and now regarded himself as untouchable in public affairs. Haman was the chief noble at the court. He was powerful and proud. He would swagger past the gate of the palace, expecting everyone to bow to him. But Mordecai refused. No doubt Mordecai had weighed the personal danger of his decision not to bow, but he had not foreseen the danger to his people.

MONOLOGUE

To say that the whole experience has served as an eye-opener for me would be a massive irony. This process hasn't been about me at all. In one sense I was just a bystander – but one who would have been crushed as surely as all the others if the evil had actually flowered.

I had always just assumed that if I personally lived as I should as a believer and ensured that I did my job in a way that honoured God, then that would be enough. Undeniably, I enjoyed the trappings and privileges that went with life at court. And I pretty much excelled in what I did, so I was always popular with Xerxes. And, behind the scenes, I sought to act in a way that was preferential to God's people. I mean, I introduced Esther to the court in a way that led to her becoming queen. Surely that was enough?

In other circumstances it would have been.

There are several things that can change a person. Consistent good fortune, a serious accident, falling in love. . . these can all change how you behave, but not much comes close to being about to die. Not so much if it happens in a fleeting moment, but if you have a number of hours, or even a number of days, to contemplate your own mortality, it reaches inside you and changes who you are. But multiply that effect by tens of thousands when you are faced with the extermination of your entire people, and by millions when you realise that you may be able to prevent it. At that point even saving your own life becomes secondary to the enormous momentum of destiny that just takes over, propelling you to actions you would have found unthinkable even a few days before.

I never liked or trusted Haman. The man had an ego the size and power of an entire army, while at the same time being so small and petty that he could feel slighted over the most incidental event. It came as no surprise to me when he inveigled his way into Xerxes' favour so far that a decree was made to have him publicly honoured on a daily basis.

It was unwarranted. He had done nothing, absolutely nothing, to earn such an honour. I have seen men at court exaggerate their accomplishments to impress the king. I've seen men take credit for other men's work. But when a man is honoured completely gratuitously, it does horrific things to his psyche.

He begins to imagine that he deserves praise simply for existing. And as I see it, it is only God whose effortless being is praiseworthy. Once you assume the position of God in your own thinking, you become an ogre. You may just become the bane of the lives of those around you, but you could equally become a genocidal maniac. And that's what happened to Haman.

But what happened to me through that time was intensely, and agonisingly, painful. To describe it as a growing-up time would be to gloss over the dealings of God in my life. I questioned so much of what I thought I knew.

Generally, it is a good rule never to doubt the things which you knew to be true when it was light just because it has become dark. The darkness that threatened to engulf our land at that time never caused me to waver in my faith in God. But with devastating effect it dismantled my view of myself.

Why had I been so adamant over the issue with Haman? Was it principle or pride? Had I thrust Esther into the path that eventually led to her becoming queen for her sake or for mine? Had I ever really considered whether my actions could be detrimental to the lives of those I loved? Is it true that I have always known best?

And this was no casual musing, no careless reflection. These thoughts cut into my brain like a razor.

It cleared my thinking enough to begin to see the purposes of God in what was happening. I realised that royal associations would not be enough to save us from rampant evil. Just burying our heads in our own lives wouldn't save us.

When I was a child we'd play a game where one of us counted and the rest of us hid. When the countdown was finished, the call would go out, 'I've counted. Coming, ready or not.'

Well, that's how it was. The countdown to the day of evil had been finished. Now it was coming for us all. Ready or not.

Of course God is sovereign. Of course deliverance for his people could have arisen from any place. But in his purposes we were all where we were, and Esther had come to royal position for such a time as this.

And in the end, it was Esther's faith and courage that brought about the situation that saved us all.

20 Esther

BACKSTORY

Esther's family had been among those of the southern kingdom of Judah captured by the Babylonians under King
Nebuchadnezzar. After the Babylonians were later conquered by the Persians under King Cyrus, the Jews were
permitted to return to Jerusalem. Esther is one of many
who chose not to return. Orphaned at a young age, she was
raised by her older cousin, Mordecai, who worked in the
household of Xerxes, the Persian king. Her age at the time
of these events is unclear. Esther is usually assumed to have
been about 16, a virginal young woman, but she may have
been a mature adult. She was strong, smart and beautiful
and had a self-assured demeanour. Originally instructed by
Mordecai to keep her identity and Jewish lineage strictly to
herself, ultimately she chose to put herself in danger when
she had nothing personally to gain.

MONOLOGUE

Everyone was shocked by what happened with Queen
Vashti. It's almost unheard of for any wife to defy her husband so openly, but the wife of Xerxes. . .

All right. I know Xerxes was very drunk. My uncle

Mordecai was there that night. And like most men, when he's drunk he can be insensitive, uncouth and even downright boorish at times. I should know. I'm his queen now. But I wouldn't even *think* that in public.

These last few years of my life have been a tumultuous procession of randomly connected events.

I wasn't really ready for Uncle Mordecai's suggestion that I should join Xerxes' harem in the hope of becoming his queen. I mean, who wants to be one of a few hundred women, some of whom haven't even seen him since the day after they came to the palace? It can be a very lonely life. It was quite a time before it suddenly felt like something I should do.

And then, when he said he wanted me to be his queen, I didn't know what to think. It was as if it wasn't really happening. I was too stunned to feel privileged, or amazed, or even overwhelmed by how rich and powerful I had just become. I certainly wasn't sure I was in love. Strangely, I am now. He can be so charming. . . except when he's drunk. But at the time it all felt so quick, like arriving at the peak of a mountain to admire the view without having to experience the arduous climb first.

The arduous climb came next.

The news, when it came, was as devastating as an earthquake. One of the few things that I had thought of as a certainty had shifted. It was as if the very law itself had changed, as if the very law of Persia had been rearranged.

'Mordecai is at the gates wearing torn clothes, sackcloth and ashes. And he's wailing at the top of his voice.'

What? Uncle Mordecai?

I had never even seen him distressed before. All those little sayings that he taught me as a child came rushing back:

'You'll never get ahead if you keep losing yours' and 'When your boat's full of water, it's better to bail than to wail'.

That Uncle Mordecai?

And when I finally got his explanation, it was worse. He sent me a messenger who showed me the text of the edict for the annihilation of all Jews and urged me to go into the king's presence to beg for mercy and plead with him.

What? Could this be the same Uncle Mordecai who used to say, 'Why plead when you can lead?', who taught me 'When you are getting on, everyone else will get on board'?

You said if I became queen, we would all be better off. You said, 'If you can get the tide to rise for you, all of us will float a little higher.' What happened to that, eh?

I sent back that message and added, 'The king hasn't asked to see me for days. You know the law. It's certain death if I go in to him unbidden, unless he extends the sceptre, beckoning me forward. All I can do is to hope the tide turns.'

Back came the message: 'That won't do any more. They've sunk our boats, all our boats, even yours. This time it isn't enough. Maybe the hand of God is what opened the door to the palace for you. Maybe it was for such a time as this. Enough of the epigrams. This is life and death. I know going in to see Xerxes could put your life in grave danger, but if you don't go in, then everyone gets to die, maybe even you. Maybe God can stop this some other way. But maybe that will be too late for you.'

I'd never heard him talk that way before. It shook me. After thinking and praying for hours, I sent him this message: 'OK. Please pray for me.

'Please fast. Tell all the people of God throughout Susa that I do this for them. Ask them all to pray and fast. I and my maids will do the same. After three days, I will go to see him.

'I know that it is illegal and I could die. I have never done something that made me this afraid before. And if I die, I die.'

I guess that could have been the end of the story, but it wasn't.

Xerxes was actually pleased that I'd come. He said that he would grant any request that I wanted to make. Still, it took me two days till I got together enough courage to say that I was unhappy with one of his decrees.

Uncle Mordecai said to me later that this event has changed him. And I know it has changed me.

I always saw life as a series of opportunities. And it is. But now I've come to see that life is more than that. It is precious. I have found a new peace in God, an answer to the persistent restlessness that used to drive me. The odd thing is that giving up my life for God has made it much richer than when I was always wanting things in my life from God.

The Sign of Jonah

The book of Jonah has four people or groups of people in it: God, Jonah, the mariners and the Ninevites. These monologues allow three people to tell their story of how God dealt with them. Reading the book of Jonah will give you all the background to the three monologues.

21 A mariner

BACKSTORY

His girlfriend: 'Romance can be a double-edged knife. Just the thought of him makes me really happy. But the other night, his first night working as a mariner, when that really horrendous storm came out of nowhere, I was really scared. And then the storm just seemed to stop. And he comes back with some tale about a man trying to run from his God. I didn't think that was possible. Listening to his story, I think I was right.'

MONOLOGUE

I've lived in Joppa all my life – growing up, finding work, first in the docks and later as part of a ship-building outfit. We're a ship-building town, and being in between Tyre and Jerusalem, an awful lot of trade comes through here.

It's a beautiful town. Its name actually means 'beauty'. For a lot of people, Joppa is synonymous with trade, but for me it is just a beautiful and romantic place to live.

Of course, the traders don't object to the romance of the town. They just can't see the point. But for me, well, beauty is not a bonus. I don't have to own every beautiful thing in order to appreciate its beauty. For me, a life without beauty is empty and devoid of soul. Sometimes I just wander along the coast, alone with my thoughts, overawed by the sheer grandeur of God. Sometimes it is all so beautiful that it scares me.

Of course the other guys in the shipyard wouldn't see it that way. But that's their problem. I don't think they really see it any way – don't think they see it at all.

But the other day I met someone else who sees it. And she is beautiful. She has a serene beauty in her manner, but she is also gorgeous to look at. I still can't quite believe she noticed me, but she did.

Her father owns several trading ships, and she got me a job on one of them.

'Can't have you building ships all your life,' she said. 'You need to work on them. That's where the romance is.' And she gave that funny little laugh of hers. I wonder what she will make of all that's happened when I tell her.

So this is where my adventure begins. Nearly where it ends.

The stranger was a tall man with a 'not-quite-safe' look, if you know what I mean. Not that he looked crazed or dangerous in the conventional sense – just unpredictable. And believe me, nothing he touched turned out predictable.

I have wondered since why he picked our boat. There were easily a dozen lined up on the harbour wall. We certainly weren't the most imposing ship, or the fastest. But we were certainly going to the most obscure place. Perhaps that was the point – ambiguity, anonymity. I guess he just didn't want to be found.

So we set off. Routine. My first time working on a ship, but routine for all that. And routine would have been quite OK for my first trip.

But it got stormy. Just a bit choppy at first, then seriously rough. Then scary. Then terrifying. I really thought we would die. We threw all the cargo into the sea to lighten the ship and then we prayed. Even if you don't believe in God, you pray at a moment like that.

And after what happened next, I don't think there's any of us that don't believe.

The captain found the stranger in a deep sleep. From the look on the other men's faces, I would say that what he did next was quite out of character. He woke him, slapping him quite violently. 'We're going to die!' he yelled. 'How can you sleep? Get up! Pray to whatever you call god!'

The crew had also got desperate, resorting to casting lots to find out who was jinxed. And the lot fell to the stranger. Some of them grabbed him. 'What have you done? Who are you? Where do you come from? What country? What people?'

Considering the ferocity of the storm, not to mention the ferocity of the questioners, he answered remarkably calmly, 'I am a Hebrew, and I worship the God of everything.'

What followed was even more remarkable. By now, even the really old hands were spooked. A kind of supernatural presence seemed to pervade the ship. You really felt that Something or Someone was doing this to us. The storm seemed to have an unnatural rage, seemed to be filled with anger, as though it had been defied.

The questions came again: 'What have you done? What should we do to make this stop?'

'Indirectly, this is my doing. I was trying to escape from God. Throw me overboard,' said the stranger, still unnervingly calm.

At first the men wouldn't hear of it. 'Everyone prays in a

storm, but I don't hold with murder. Apart from anything else, killing a man at sea is bound to get us all cursed.' And they tried to row back to shore. But the sea grew even wilder and the wind even fiercer.

In the end most of the crew thought it was our only hope. And so, with much trepidation and uncertainty, two of the men threw him overboard. Inasmuch as the situation allowed, he was dignified and calm to the end. But no one really expected what came next.

The wind dropped, but that sometimes happens suddenly. The unbelievable thing was the way the sea became instantly calm, almost as though it had absorbed the calmness of the stranger.

And then, while we were all just staring at the water in amazement, a huge sea creature broke its surface. It looked like an enormous fish, and it raced across the water and swallowed the stranger in a single gulp.

Then the sea was utterly still. For about an hour after that we all stood in silent disbelief, shocked and traumatised by what we had just witnessed. We stared across the water, stretching before us so motionless it could have been a sheet of beaten metal, in futile straining to see the stranger re-emerge. In the end we started to row for the shore, the only disturbance being to the surface of our life, our angst unexpressed.

I don't know what it all meant. But for me, beauty is more than ever something to be thankful for, and God in his grandeur is Someone to be feared.

22 Jonah

The Bible treats the story of Jonah as historical fact. Apart from the book attributed to him, Jonah is mentioned only once in the Old Testament, in 2 Kings 14:25, where it is stated that the restoration by Jeroboam II of the borders of Israel against the incursions of foreign invaders was a fulfilment of the 'word of the Lord the God of Israel, which he spoke by his servant Jonah'. Jesus referred to 'the sign of Jonah', by which he meant that his being swallowed by a fish for three days was also a remarkable sign pointing to the death and resurrection of Christ, presaging the event that the prophet himself never really understood.

MONOLOGUE

The ship had the figurehead of a bird. That's why I chose it. A huge, angry, hungry-looking bird. It seemed to sum up how I was feeling. Racing across the water, its wings flung back behind it, its mouth open, ready to shriek, ready to devour its prey.

I didn't want to go to Nineveh. The Assyrians are a cruel, godless race. But their star seems to be in the ascendant. Within a generation they will be a serious threat to us. Why should I care if they are destroyed? And why would they listen to me even if I did?

Choosing a ship to take me away from them seemed like the only thing I could do. And for the first hour I really believed I could do it. And then the storm came. Initially slowly, but then it hit us with a vengeance. At first I was below in my cabin asleep, resigned to my impotence in the face of whatever God was doing. But then the captain woke me, yelling that we all needed to pray.

The wind was like nothing I'd ever experienced before, screaming at us from every direction, sounding like the screams of a demented woman. The waves raced down upon us like great angry monsters. The lightning lit up the sky and the thunder boomed as the storm attacked our helpless ship with all its fury. The hull creaked and groaned with the strain that the ship was taking as she leaped and danced in this typhoon. We were lifted half out of the water, and when we hit the water again it was with such force that we went right under. The mounting chaos gave way to total pandemonium.

For a minute the crew seemed to be paralysed with fear, unable to do anything but pray, and I alone knew that it would be futile. I alone knew that I was to blame, and that no amount of prayer could change that. God had decided this as a consequence of my disobedience. The crew had thrown all the cargo overboard, to no avail. It was me that they needed to jettison if they were to live.

The moment came when they had to do that, and they took some persuading (I kept thinking, how unlike the Assyrians that I had been sent to). I really didn't know what to expect, but nothing prepared me for the ordeal to come.

The shock of the icy water lasted just a moment, and then

I was lifted into the mouth of some creature, and I felt myself slipping down what I know must have been its throat. The sensation only lasted a short time, and I found myself to be in a slightly larger chamber. It was pitch black. I reached out to feel where I was, and my hands came in contact with a soft, slimy material that seemed to pull away from my hand when I touched it. In the end it dawned on me that I must have been swallowed by a sea creature. The sensation was horrifying. It seemed to open the very pores of my skin, drawing out my strength.

Desperation brings a certain focus to your life. I wondered if this was going to be how I died. My prayer had always been that I would do something supremely significant, pointing men to the promised Messiah. I didn't want my life's calling to be to avert judgement from a group of godless pagans. But right now, even that felt as though it could be enough.

I realised that God in his goodness plans the very detail of our lives, and that my aspirations, where they differed from his, had become idols themselves.

I was hurled into the deep, into the very heart of the creature, and the currents swirled about me. All God's waves and breakers swept over me till I felt that even he couldn't see me.

I imagined how it would feel to see him.

With my dying breath, water swirling all around me, seaweed wrapped round my head, and trapped in this tomb, I imagined how it would feel to see him. What would I say?

By clinging to worthless idols we so easily lose our grip on grace. I could feel my life ebbing away, sinking without a trace.

I lost consciousness more than once. The final time that I

came round I realised I was hungry. I had no idea how long it had been. With no night, no day and nothing happening apart from the creature occasionally belching and heaving, I had no way to gauge the time. The creature was obviously not enjoying the experience any more than I was.

Suddenly it became really agitated, convulsing and thrashing about. At that moment I was sure I would die, but then suddenly I was catapulted into the light. Out of my distress I had called to God, and he had heard me. From this living tomb I called for help, and he listened to my cry. I called out to him, and he answered me. He rescued me. I was outside, alive and breathing fresh air.

This is my song. He saved me. I'm not sure where I am, but, wherever I am, I will go to Nineveh.

23 A Ninevite

BACKSTORY

Nineveh was one of the largest cities of its time, and it was the enemy of the Israelites. The Assyrians were already raiding the frontiers, and they were a byword for cruelty and ruthlessness. Only about 50 years after Jonah's visit they attacked and conquered the northern kingdom of Israel. Within another hundred years, the prophet Nahum tells us, Nineveh had fully returned to its old ways, and even exceeded them. He says Nineveh 'plots evil against the LORD and counsels wickedness' as well as causing 'many casualties, piles of dead, bodies without number, people stumbling over the corpses – all because of the wanton lust of a harlot, alluring, the mistress of sorceries, who enslaved nations by her prostitution and peoples by her witchcraft'.

MONOLOGUE

Nineveh is a feisty city. Everyone has opinions about everything. People can argue about the time of day. I've seen brawls over who's got the best idol, and fights to the death if someone is sleeping with someone else's woman. Cheating in the market is practically *de rigueur*, as is the tirade of foul-mouthed abuse that gets issued when the cheat is uncovered.

If you want to live here, be aware that patience, understanding and compassion are all in short supply. It's not advisable to live here if your face doesn't fit. Don't be poor. Don't get old, and definitely don't get sick. Don't be foreign. Don't be a widow. Don't expect anyone to help you up if you fall. Expect to fight for everything you get, and remember: men have been killed over a look.

At least it used to be like that – until a few days ago. Who knows any more?

A few days. But what a few days. On Tuesday a man comes up out of the sea. Some of the stories about how he got here are wild.

A giant sea-fish beaches itself on the shore. It lies there motionless for half an hour and then suddenly starts squirming and writhing, convulsing and thrashing about until, with one almighty retch, it vomits up a man, or at least something that may once have been a man. His appearance is disgusting. His hair is matted and entangled with weed and small fishbones. His clothes are full of holes. His skin looks as though all the life has been drained from it, sickly white and wrinkled like poor leather. He has wild eyes and wheezes as he breathes. When he speaks, it is painful to listen to his rasping, fraught tones, although it is also utterly compelling. He was covered in a vile-smelling slime when he emerged. At least he washed the worst of that off.

But that was all he did. Making no real attempt to make himself presentable, he sets off to get into the heart of the city, running as though he has to do something urgent. But when he gets there, all he does is shout.

'Forty more days and Nineveh will be destroyed!' That's it. Eight words. Over and over. Again and again. Endlessly repeating the same thing. No attempt to explain. No promise of the chance of reprieve. Just this persistence, this mesmerising rant.

At times it sounds as though he is gloating, promising devastation with a wild smile. Who is he, this fish man, this feral prophet? Are his words supposed to haunt us or taunt us?

But something else has started to happen. Unplanned. Unannounced. But not unnoticed.

People have started to get together. At first it was impromptu chats on street corners. Now it is vast gatherings in the open spaces within and outside the city. No longer just chats. Compunction is the order of the day, remorse seeping from our very pores. Gone is the sassy city. Contrition replaces aggression. The make-believe world where sensuality could pose as spirituality is crumbling. Our pretensions are dying. Already there have been several bonfires of idols and fetishes. People have started wearing sackcloth.

By the third day the news has reached the king. In foregone days the messenger would have been made into body parts, fed to the fishes where he came from. But not now. Mourning is mandated. Our statues of deities replaced with a statute for piety.

Day three ends. The herald departs. Some say he has gone east to await the arrival of a destroying army, but none comes. Gradually consternation gives way to celebration.

By Saturday the pervasive conviction and anticipation of death that gripped us all has given way to a carnival of life. In foregone days it would have been an excuse for uncontrolled debauchery, but now there's only unrestrained praise to the God who has spared us.

*The Star – How the Nativity Touched
Ordinary Lives*

24 The shepherd

BACKSTORY

Most of us are familiar with the story of Herod killing all the baby boys in Bethlehem, but maybe we're so familiar with it that we never really stop to consider the lives that were devastated by the event, and what effect it had on them in later years when they encountered the man Jesus Christ. Read Luke 2:8–16 and Matthew 2:13–16 to get the background to this story.

MONOLOGUE

Well, I guess you want to hear about when I saw the Bethlehem child. They always do, especially at this time of year. 'Were there really angels?' 'Was he really in a manger?' Always the same questions. Well, yes. There were angels, shepherds, cows, sheep, two young people and a baby.

But that's not the half of it. You see, three times that Bethlehem child has changed my life, and I'm old enough to be his father. In fact, that first night I reckoned I was a bit older than his folks. It was a magical evening. Oh, it started like any other – sitting on a hillside, watching the sheep, complaining about the cold and teasing Jacob, the youngest of the lads, who had just got married. First night he had slept away from home, if you get my drift. Anyhow, we see this man approaching, on foot, but he's tall. Over six feet. And when he reaches us, he asks, 'Do you know what the word "Messiah" means?' Everybody laughs. 'Course we do. He is the promised prince, the one who will lead our people to freedom.'

'Well,' says the man, in a very commanding tone, 'he's here. Just down the road. You will see him tonight.' You could have heard a pin drop. It never occurred to me not to believe him, even before the others appeared. Suddenly, there's hundreds, maybe thousands, all around us. Appeared from nowhere. All singing. Music to break the heart of the hardest cynic. Made you want to dance, and cry, and laugh, and love everyone and everything.

But I didn't dance – I ran. Down the road where the first man had pointed. Right up to the edge of town. And from the bottom of an outbuilding, where there should be nothing but cows, there's a baby crying. Well, I just had to look. And there's this young couple. He's grinning from ear to ear. She just looks tired, but happy. And there's this little baby. Not six hours old. But his folks don't yell at me. They smile. 'Have you come to see him?' says the man. And before I can say, 'What, in here?', I realise he's talking about the baby. 'You can hold him,' he says. Well, my first kid is due any day, so I figure, 'What's the harm?' But when I reach out my hand, that's when it happens.

Suddenly I'm overcome. I can hardly stand. And I get this feeling, like all the music I had heard on the hillside was about this baby. Before I know it, I'm on my knees. By now the others have caught me up, and I think they feel it too, 'cos they're all on their knees.

I don't how long it was before the man put the child in a

manger, and the moment passed. We went back to the hillside and never spoke another word till morning.

The next week my son was born, to my darling Rebecca. I've never been so happy. My son. Born into the same world as the Bethlehem child. I felt the world would never be the same. My son would grow up in the same world as him. I didn't know what it all meant, but I knew it was the best. They were dreamlike days – Rebecca singing around the house, the night watches with the lads. No more complaining about the cold, just talking about that night, like we felt special, chosen.

[Pause]

Then the horror began. One day like any other. But this day, Herod's men ride into town, and there's a lot of yelling and screaming, and I run out of the house, and I'm knocked down by some thug who puts a sword to my neck, and two of his mates kick open the door. I can hear my Rebecca screaming, but I can't move. And the men come out, and they've got my boy. But he's not crying. He's dead. And soon, it's the same in every house, right through the town. They killed every boy in the place, and just rode away, like it was all in a day's work.

[Pause]

That night, my Rebecca's hair, her beautiful, dark-brown hair, went white. Not grey – white. In one day. And then my skin went white. I hid it for a bit, but it just spread. 'Leprosy,' the priest said, and that was it. I was banished from the village. I lived 30 years on my own. How do you explain that? I saw heaven and hell within the space of eight weeks.

And I lived that hell for another 30 years. I used to lie awake, planning how to kill Herod, till I heard he had died a couple of years afterwards. After that I just used to lie awake and feel dead inside.

Then, one day, I hear the Carpenter is in town. Jesus, they call him. And the word is he has a cure for leprosy. So I go. What's to lose?

Now, I swear this next bit is true. No word of a lie, this is what I saw. I'm planning on just turning up and seeing what happens. And then I see the man. And I know. As God is my witness, I know that he is the Bethlehem child. Don't ask me how I knew, I just did. I could hear that music again. Inside me. And I know it's about him. And I'm on my knees again. And I hear myself saying, 'Please! I know that if you want to, you can make me clean.' And he says, 'I do want to. Be clean.' And he touches my head. First time I've been touched in 30 years. And suddenly I realise. I know he's the Bethlehem child. And he knows I'm the shepherd. Like he recognises me from that night, if that were possible. And he says, 'Be clean.' And that music reaches down inside me, and wrings me out, like you wring last night's dew out of a cloth. Wrings out all my hatred of those men. Wrings out all the nights I prayed to die. Wrings out all the days I missed my Rebecca and my son so much I thought I would die. And I feel clean inside. And I look at my hands, and they're clean. So are my feet, my arms, my chest. I am clean. And then he smiles.

[Pause]

But that's not quite the end. I'll tell you something that'll make you laugh out loud. Last week, in the Temple market,

I heard two of the priests saying that this Jesus is trouble. 'What's to be done?' they were saying. And one of them answered, 'It's him or us. We've got to rid Jerusalem of him. We've got to bury him.'

Well, here's what I think. Do you reckon you could dig a hole big enough to bury Mount Zion? Do think that Caesar could order a tower so high that a man could pile rocks on the sun till it sank below the waves? Do you think a whole army could bury the Great Sea in the sand? Even if you could do all this, I will tell you the only thing I know. That man has the whole of heaven inside him. He might let them arrest him, if it suits him. He might even let them kill him, just to prove this point: even if you can lose a mountain, sink the sun and fill in the sea you will never, ever, ever bury him. I know. I've known him for 30 years.

25 One of the Magi

BACKSTORY

We often think about there being three kings who came to see the baby Jesus. But Scripture doesn't say they were kings, and it doesn't say there were three of them. They were magi, Eastern mystics. They brought three gifts, but the earliest stories and paintings of them show any number of them, possibly even a dozen. Reading Matthew 2:1–12 will give you the background to this story.

MONOLOGUE

The unknown is the appeal. To be one of the magi makes you a poet, philosopher, historian and storyteller. It makes you part of a nation's soul. Sometimes a story is too good not to be true. It is not supposed to be just smoke and mirrors. We've got too adept at making everything vague and palatable, saying what's wanted instead of what's true.

I haven't travelled all this time because I knew what I'd find, but because I didn't know. Undemanding answers are for demanding children. In this way we pass our grasp of life on to our children. We develop our understanding of life early and rarely deviate from it, but what happens when life deviates from our understanding? What happens when the ground begins to shift below us? Once we begin to accumulate explanations for our lives, we don't welcome news that disturbs them. We protect ourselves from whatever grain of truth we think will cause discomfort. We embrace confirmation of our ideas and shun contradiction.

So what if a new star creeps across our skies? Who notices? Who cares? This is a story of life's magic and wonder – if you will hear it.

Nobody believes us. Now we're back, nobody believes us. Nobody understands why we have spent two years away from home, family, comfort and security. A magi's instinct should be to search for truth. Surely they can't always have been this parsimonious? Years of flattery has left them with dilapidated egos. Their days are spent reinforcing each other's prejudices. The quest has left their spirits. They wanted us to return with things. A few honours, a treasure chest or two, even a new alliance would have silenced our critics. But we have given them a mystery instead.

We saw him. We left here telling them we were going in search of a king, and we found him. It wasn't what we expected. He wasn't who we expected. He certainly wasn't where we expected. But that's where the beauty of the story lies.

We went to Herod's palace expecting him to be there. We presumed we would find an infant prince, born into splendour and destined to ascend Herod's throne. Instead, we found indolence and ignorance. After seeing an endless procession of court officials, all of whom had nothing to say, we were finally treated to Herod putting on a display of obsequiousness, imploring us to return when we had found the child. I mistrusted the man. The scribes here said we should go to a town called Bethlehem, because of ancient writings that foretell a divine king coming from there.

It's not a large town, and as we reached it we saw the first few meagre houses straggling along the road of our approach. Suddenly we all felt like going to one of these peasant homes, although why I can't really say. I honestly cannot recall seeing a more unlikely place for royalty, throughout our entire journey. I went to the home first, for fear that if we all went we might overwhelm the occupants, but, despite the incongruous nature of the visit, they seemed unsurprised and welcomed us in.

We talked for quite a while. Theirs was an unlikely tale, which sounds more inconceivable every time you tell it, but they themselves were charming. If I have never been in such an insubstantial house before, I have certainly never met such a couple. They had a genuine and amiable charisma. They were at ease with us and with themselves. Their story was as overpowering as they themselves were unassuming.

The girl had been a young virgin, engaged to be married to the young man. She described an encounter with an angelic being who announced that her destiny was to carry the child who would ultimately be their king. She questioned this as premature. She was as yet unmarried. The angel said that all this was to be miraculous.

What followed was a long story about their faith, their love, the scandal of their perceived circumstances, oppression by the Romans (who appear to have forced the entire country to relocate to help them collect taxes) and mysterious encounters with a gang of shepherds, a couple of ageing prophets and, lastly, us. There was much that was memorable in what they told us, but one part of their story has burnt its way into me.

In one of their encounters with the prophetic there was

a man who told the young woman, 'This child is destined to cause the falling and rising of many. And also a sword will pierce your own soul.' As she told this part, her voice quivered, and it was the first time in this whole incredible story, so full of glory and hardship, that I saw tears in her eyes.

Once they had told the story, they woke the child to show him to us. I have never before been overawed by anyone, but the realisation that this little, babbling infant was destined to be a king floored me. It floored every one of us, and we all spent time in quiet adoration of the child and his God.

Then I remembered that before we left we had purchased gifts for the king – gold and some royal fragrances. We gave them to the couple. They were astounded at the gold. I don't think they had ever held any before. They seemed to understand something from the frankincense, but as I reached to give them the myrrh I almost held back. We had learned since arriving there that in that part of the world it was not just an oil of beauty but was also used to embalm the dead, and suddenly it seemed an inappropriate gift for such a happy and holy moment.

They received it as graciously as everything else they had done since we met them. But for the second time I saw the young woman's eyes fill with tears.

26 The innkeeper's wife

BACKSTORY

Joseph and Mary's failure to find anywhere to stay was not because the locals were inhospitable or heartless. But an extra two (or even three) people were an inconvenience that few could afford. The inns were overfull throughout Israel because of the Roman emperor's decree that everyone be counted and taxed. Inns were private businesses, and those in Bethlehem were no exception. But in the midst of this we hear a story from the owners of one inn. There is no mention of the innkeeper even charging the couple. It's astonishing, then, to think that in this world-changing event, the birth of Jesus, God was served by the unnamed owners of this inn. Reading Luke 2:1–12 will give you the background to this story.

MONOLOGUE

There's never a dull moment here in this home, always people passing through, needing a place to stop. And you hear such stories, although I'm sure that half of them can't be true. Mind you, my husband always says that you could believe that some of the people who stay here were made up if you hadn't actually met them. Travellers, soldiers, traders and sailors – some running from life and others looking for it.

But there was one year that beat all the others hands down for sheer variety. Across the years that I have done this I have never met so many people, so many beautiful, tragic, rich, dull, mischievous, troubled, lazy, passionate, annoying or downright kooky people, in such a few months.

It was the year of the great Roman taxation. Wherever you were, you had to return to the town of your birth. Several of the women whose husbands ran inns used to meet over lunch every now and then to swap stories. We even had a competition for the most unusual story, but we could put one forward only if we had actually seen it with our own eyes.

Well, one week the prize went to the story of a man who claimed to be a trader in fine cloth but had the roughest hands, clothes and manners you ever saw. Another week it went to the story of a deserting soldier trying to pass himself off as a local but knowing only three words in Aramaic: 'please', 'toilet' and 'camel'. We never did find out if he made it back home. But my best story and, to my mind, the best story of that entire year, was the one about the shepherds, the baby and the manger.

Imagine having to travel all the way from Nazareth to Bethlehem. Now imagine that the roads are heaving with travellers. Add to it that you're nine months pregnant and cap it off by finding you've got nowhere to stay. Now you've got a picture of the rather heartbreaking sight that greeted me when someone knocked one night. And they were both so young! He looked so earnest, and she, well, she just looked big. Big and tired. They said that she hadn't slept in a bed or eaten a hot meal for days.

Well, I hadn't got a bed. I've always tried to keep our private life separate from our livelihood, but I would have let them sleep in our own room, only my husband's brother was staying with us, and he and his wife were already asleep. I felt so sorry for her – well, for both of them, really. They looked exhausted, and I was sure she was going to have that baby at any minute, right there in the street if I didn't get them inside somewhere. So I took them to where the animals were. It was newly done out, and it was warm and dry. It wasn't that long ago that we used to have all the animals in with us, like many folks do.

I just got the couple fresh straw to sleep on, but soon she went into labour. I was worried that she was too tired to be able to have the baby, and it turned out it was her first. Well, you may have been there at the birth for a dozen friends and family, but it still doesn't really prepare you for the first one of your own. She had no one she knew in the town, so I said I would stay with her.

Mercifully it was remarkably quick. When I asked her what she was hoping for, she kept saying 'It will be a boy' over and over. Well, I've seen labour have that effect on women before, making them say strange things. At my niece's birth my sister suddenly announced that she had changed her mind about having the baby at all!

Well, this time it turned out that the young woman was right – she had a beautiful baby boy. Once I had got mother and baby cleaned up and settled, the three of them looked so happy and so sleepy that I confess I got quite misty-eyed.

The next problem was where to put the baby. I was just wondering who might have an old crib and who also wouldn't mind being woken up at that time of night, when the new dad took the baby from his wife and put him in an old manger from the corner of the room.

It seemed a good time for all of us to get some sleep, when I heard an almighty commotion. It was a bunch of shepherds, all of them looking like ruffians and most of them with manners to match. Well, one came in all cocky, and then the others followed.

'Oh no you don't,' I said. 'You wait outside. I don't know what you want here, anyway.' And I picked up a broom to hit them with, but suddenly they were all on their knees. At any other time it would have looked hysterical, but actually it was quite moving. I heard one of them say, 'It's just like he said. The baby was in a manger.' They stayed that way for about an hour, and then they just left, filed out in the most emotional silence. But the most astonishing thing was the way the couple reacted, almost as if they were expecting them.

Well, a few days later the couple just left. They wanted to go to Jerusalem to make the customary sacrifice for a new-born child. They thanked me before they left, but they wouldn't be drawn into explaining the incident with the shepherds. All she would say was that she thought they were lovely and that she would treasure the memory.

I still say that all shepherds are louts, and I can't think of anything that they could do that could ever be anyone's treasured memory. Although that couple and that baby probably are my favourite memory from that year.

27 The story of Anna

BACKSTORY

Luke doesn't tell us much about Simeon and Anna. He doesn't even say whether they knew each other. But we can tell they were devout. We know Simeon had been watching all his life in anticipation that he would see the Messiah. We know Anna had lost her husband after just seven years of marriage and used the rest of her life to pray and fast. Sometimes God can take his time preparing you for what can seem like something fleeting, even insignificant to most. Anna's inclusion in the Christmas story gives this little old lady one of the most awe-inspiring walk-on parts in history. Reading Luke 2:21–38 will give you the background.

MONOLOGUE

Her name was Anna, Anna bar-Phanuel, that old lady from the Temple. Everyone recognised her, but hardly anyone knew her name.

Over 50 years she had been there. Part of the furniture, you might say. Fifty years. For some folk, she would form part of their earliest memory of a Temple visit. There in the background, helping and serving, fetching and carrying, running errands for the priests, but mostly just worshipping and praying. For some she would be the last face they saw here before they died. And for some she could even be both. From the cradle to the grave, a consistent witness to all of the faithfulness of God. She was 84, you know. Imagine that – 84!

If you looked, you would always see her somewhere in the Temple, often tucked away in a quiet corner. I could usually find her, hidden away from most people's gaze, out of the bustle and the busy-ness of Temple life. I don't think she noticed me, but whenever I had the time I would watch her, sometimes for hours. I could see her lips moving, although I couldn't actually hear what she was saying. Sometimes I thought she must be worshipping, her whole demeanour showing awe, as though she felt herself in the presence of something or someone great. And sometimes I thought she must be praying, her face a picture of concentration, sometimes laughing, sometimes weeping, always a portrait of the beauty of dedication. I always remember watching her. You felt that she silently ushered you into the presence of God.

Some days there used to be an old boy here as well, Simon, who used to do the same. He wasn't here as often, but when he was, you could always sense the presence of God.

No, it wasn't Simon.

[Pause]

Simeon. That was it. Simeon. I used to think he was a rather austere character. But then again, I didn't really know him. I had a long chat with him once, and after that he would always greet me with a smile.

And then, there was that day.

They just looked like an ordinary couple to me, young parents such as you could see any day at the Temple. The law requires you to make an offering whenever a child is born. Usually it's a lamb, but if you're poor it can just be birds, for example, a pair of pigeons or turtledoves.

And this couple looked poor. They must have travelled quite a long way just to get to the Temple. They didn't look that tired, but their shoes looked very worn, and their clothes were quite threadbare. And the baby was just wrapped up in an old cloth.

Anyway, they had obviously just come from making a sacrifice (I bet it was only a pair of birds) when all of a sudden old Simeon came up to them. And then Anna came. I never got to hear what Simeon said, but the couple looked a little overawed, and Anna had that face she sometimes does when she's been praying for hours.

Suddenly Anna called out, like she expected everyone in the Temple to stop whatever they were doing and to listen to her. And by and large everyone did just that. I'm not sure that I'd ever heard her speak before.

She had a voice that I would describe as soft. Not quiet. Not quiet at all, especially when you think how old she was. I'm sure everyone heard her that day, but it was a soft, gentle, warming kind of voice. And an excited voice. She sounded as if she had real news to tell.

She asked everyone first if they could see that the city needed a move of God. Well, that wasn't a particularly hard one. Bit of a no-brainer, really.

We've got all the outward trappings of religion. In fact, I reckon that we're the most religious city on earth. After all, this is the city of God. Of course you hear about bigger cities from the caravans of traders, but this is God's city. Ours is the glory, the covenants, the Law, the Temple. Ours is the lineage, all the way back to Abraham. I reckon we've got it all. But the tragedy is, you couldn't tell that from looking at us. The heart has gone from it all.

But Anna just warmed to her message. To listen to her speak, we must have been on the verge of the biggest revival Israel has ever seen. And she kept drawing it all back to the child that the couple were holding.

Fair dos. He was a good-looking little lad, but that was all that I could see. But to hear Anna you would have believed he was going to be the Messiah.

She spoke of a fresh wave of the presence of God. 'God has come to help his people,' she kept saying. 'God is here. He is here. To some of you that will be a blessing. To some of you it will be a curse. To all of us it will be a surprise. He will arise from where you wouldn't dream to look.'

And she nodded again in the direction of the couple.

'Prepare to be amazed. For you have longed for days past, for the golden age of David, for the wild days of Elijah. But they looked forward in anticipation of this day.'

I'm not sure what she meant, but I have never seen her so. . . so enlivened, so animated.

And it all seemed to start with that little baby. I wonder where it will end.

First Sign – The Wedding at Cana

Reading John 2:1–11 will give you a background to this story.

28 The bride

We sometimes think that a wedding today takes too much organising. Maybe so, but in first-century AD Israel, wedding ceremonies lasted a week. The Bible says this incident happened 'on the third day', thus on Tuesday. The six stone water-pots were used for ceremonial washing before meals. This was not a requirement of biblical law, but something invented by the Pharisees. How like Jesus to take legalism and bring a party to it!

MONOLOGUE

To be honest, it could have been a bit awkward. OK – it could have been downright embarrassing. Not a good start to our marriage having David made into the laughing-stock of the village. I can hear them now:

'Did you get the joke about the groom getting the wine for his wedding?'

'No. I didn't get it.'

'That's OK – neither did he!'

Or:

'What's the difference between the wine at a wedding and a bride who's embarrassed by poor catering?'

'I don't know.'

'They both run out, but only the bride runs out in tears.'

Which wouldn't really have been fair. It's not that he didn't get any. He just didn't get enough. The merchant who sold it to him said it would be enough. Maybe the merchant's friends aren't that good at partying. David's friends could party for their country, and mine treat partying like a mission from God.

We should never have listened to him. Should've trusted our own judgement. He has obviously forgotten what it's like to be young.

Anyway, the party is in full swing when the banquet master comes up to David and says, 'Excuse me, sir, but we are getting dangerously low on the wine.' And, typical David, he says, 'Don't worry, squire. Leave it to me.'

Don't know what he was thinking. I use the word 'thinking' in the loosest possible sense. Probably high on the party mood, if you get my drift.

Now, I know David's mother is a very resourceful woman. How could I not know? She tells me often enough. But not even she could find half a dozen jars of any half-decent wine on a Tuesday night.

As I say, with the party going great, and everyone else blissfully unaware of the impending drought, what was a girl to do?

I particularly remember a rowdy bunch of friends of David's family. All very good-natured, but, boy, were they rowdy! Mainly fishermen, I think, from over Galilee way. I'm sure they made a serious contribution to the party spirit, and I'm also pretty sure they contributed more than their fair share to the dent in our stash of wine.

Turns out one of them was a carpenter. But he could get

his hands on some fabulous vintage. And he didn't even want paying.

First thing David knows about it is when the banquet master comes up again and says, 'This is remarkable, sir. Everyone brings out the choice wine first and then the cheaper wine after the guests have had too much to drink; but what you've done is to keep the best till now.'

David says he wasn't sure whether it was a compliment or a criticism. Either way, that carpenter saved the day as far as we're concerned.

The thing is, there's a story going round that an hour before it was just water. Well, I can't vouch for anyone else, but I hadn't had anywhere near enough to drink to mistake water for wine. And it definitely wasn't water by the time it got to me.

The story is that one of the waiters (another fisherman by trade!) says the carpenter got him and some others to fill six stone jars with water from the well.

But I had some water from that well earlier in the day, and it wasn't all that. . . Let's just say that it wasn't all that. So how did the carpenter do it?

Some say he prayed.

Well, that's a bit much. I know there was nowhere else to get it, but it's still a bit much. I have always believed, ever since I was a child. I suppose I believe that God in his power can do whatever he pleases.

But wine at a wedding! Why would he care? Bearing in mind that even the wine merchant was too old to remember how to have a good time, are you seriously asking me to believe that God is young enough to know how to party?

29 The wine waiter (fisherman)

BACKSTORY

The wine waiter's wife: 'My husband Jacob is a simple man, but he's proud. Losing his job has been the end for him. He thinks that God has let him down. And though he has never said it, somehow he makes me feel that I have let him down, although I don't know how. I know he feels a failure as a worker, as husband, even as a man. And I don't know how much more of his cynical resentfulness against life I can stand.'

MONOLOGUE

I'm not a wine waiter. **[He has just been announced to the audience as such]** All right?

I'm a fisherman. I've always been a fisherman. My father was a fisherman, and so was his father. I was born within earshot of the fluttering of sails in a gentle breeze. My earliest childhood memory is of standing with my grandfather by the jetty while the nets of fish were landed, all gleaming silver and flapping.

It's a life full of reality. I could tell you about the time I laughed till I thought I would burst watching my brothers struggling to pull in a badly cast net, overfull with fish, until finally capsizing. Or how I wept till I thought the world would end taking back the body of a friend who drowned in a storm, wondering what there was that I could tell his wife. How do you tell two little kids that Daddy isn't coming home, ever? I wondered if there could ever be enough tears to shed for the most decent man I ever knew. And I have stood amazed and speechless while dawn broke over Lake Gennesaret. It's a privilege that leaves you feeling that you have never lived before that moment, and that you may never experience such extravagance again. And yet I have watched thousands of them.

So what am I doing here? A wine waiter at a wedding of two young social climbers, pledging to love and honour each other for better or worse. They don't know what worse is. They don't know what it is for your boss to die and his upstart of a son to tell you that he doesn't need you any more. That groom will never have to face his wife with the news that they are about to become poor, penniless and worthless. That bride will never cry herself to sleep because she can't decide whether to buy her children food or clothes.

I have wandered the streets of Kursi at night listening to the sea and wondering if in the morning it will all have drained away, like everything else I love. Whether the sun would rise in the morning and whether anyone would notice if it didn't, provided they had enough light to work by. I'll tell you what insanity is. It's when you run out of reasons to live, but still have 30 years ordained for you. It's when you look at your wife and realise you get no pleasure in love any more. It's when your kids tell you they're hungry and all you can think is, 'Don't bother me with things I can't help.' It's when you realise that praying is just worrying out loud. Insanity is when you run out of life.

And now we've run out of wine. Not just run out of good wine. That's not uncommon. By this time in the evening even the *nouveaux riches* are trotting out the cheap plonk in the hope the guests are too drunk to notice.

If I was at all bothered about this whole pretentious show, I would be outraged. Even when we had nothing to live on, we knew enough to always make a guest welcome. These people have everything, but they still scrimp on their guests.

But no. We haven't just run out of good wine. We have run out of wine full stop. End of story. The groom is going to have to tell them soon. That pompous, supercilious little man is going to have embarrass himself in front of the whole village. And I get to watch.

But first we have one last desperate act of absurdity to endure. There's a carpenter here. Now there's a good idea. We've run out of wine. Is there a wine merchant in the house? How about a vineyard owner? No, wait, I've got a better idea. Does anyone know a good carpenter?

Apparently his mother is a friend of the groom's family. And for some reason she has decided to get involved. So she walks in here and announces in a rather excited voice, 'My son has agreed to help.' Like we're supposed to be pleased. 'Do exactly what he tells you.' And with that she goes out, and he walks in.

And here's the mystery for me. He had a calm voice, a good voice. Not the sort of voice you normally associate with people who have lost touch with the planet. And he explained it very carefully, without sounding patronising. 'There are six large stone jars here. I want you to go across the square, draw water from the well and fill every jar to the brim.'

I mean, six stone jars full of water are not going to help anyone. He might as well have said, 'Fetch me six live chickens' or 'I am going to need half a dozen headbands.' Actually, I wish he had. Water is heavy, and they were big jars.

And yet – he doesn't look like the village idiot. **[Pauses and then shrugs]** I guess he must be.

Anyhow, it gets better. We've filled the jars, and now he says, 'Draw some out and take it to the master of the banquet.' Well, no one's told the banquet master yet. If anyone goes up to him with a cup, he's going to expect it to be wine. And when it isn't, he's going to dismiss the imbecile who has brought him the water. And guess who drew the short straw. . .

Actually, I'm past caring. The caterers have run out of wine. I've run out of hope, and the family have run out of ideas. The only thing we haven't run out of is mystical carpenters and their optimistic mothers. The banquet master has the cup, and in another minute I shall have the sack.

[Another, longer pause as he walks slowly to a chair and sits down, looking shocked]

This is all happening too quick for me. I know that was water. I fetched it myself. My eyes watched as I poured it into the jars. My hands held the buckets. But then my ears heard the banquet master lavishing praise on the groom for the excellence of the wine. And my mouth tasted it, and I've never tasted better.

And just now I swear I heard the carpenter's voice in my head. And he called my name. And then he said, 'Jacob! When you run out of wine, or out of hope and love and life, you can always call on me.'

30 The wine waiter's niece

Jacob's friend: 'Jacob always was a straight-up man. You know the sort. Everything is on the surface. He doesn't have hidden depths. He doesn't have hidden anything. No secret longings, no undercover agenda. What you see is what you get. So when I heard his niece recounting what he claims to have seen at the wedding, I was confused. I doubt very much that he has started seeing things, and he doesn't have it in him to make it up. The trouble is that means it has to be true.'

MONOLOGUE

Yes, I've heard the stories. All laughable. They just don't know Uncle Jake, that's all.

I mean, it's obvious. Uncle Jake a fantasist, Uncle Jake a drunk, Uncle Jake a liar? I don't think so.

I know he's not an angel. He hasn't even been a very nice person recently. But he's not any of those other things.

I've known him all my life, since I was a little kid. I always used to say he was my favourite big person, when I was growing up. He was always jolly, always joking. I think he used to drive Mum mad with his practical jokes, and she was always shouting, 'Don't you get the children worked up! It's nearly their bed time. I know you don't have any of your own yet, but that's no excuse to go spoiling my kids.' And if he was still at our house at bed time, he would tell us a story, usually about fishermen.

And then, a few years ago, he completely changed. I think something happened and he couldn't be a fisherman any more. And that was all he really cared about. That and Leah, his wife. And probably Dad and Mum, and us kids.

Mum and Dad said they didn't even recognise him any more. He became very bitter, and angry and cynical. And no one liked being around him. But he never turned to drink. He always said that kind of person was weak, and getting drunk showed no respect for yourself or anyone else. He never changed on that. And he always said that there was no one whom he so wanted to impress that it was worth lying about anything. Actually, that did change a bit. He used to say, 'Why should I care what anyone thinks? They can all think anything they like. I'm going to say it how it is. And I don't care if it upsets them all.'

It's a nastier way of saying it, but I guess it means the same.

But now so much has changed again. He's still a cynic. Still jokes about everything as if he didn't care about anything. But the antagonism has gone. He's got the twinkle back in his eye. He notices other people again. He's appreciative. I know he's still having to work as a wine waiter when all he really wants to do is get back to fishing, but at least he's got work. The other day I heard him telling someone that if he hadn't lost his fishing job, he would never have been at that wedding that day and never met Jesus, and that meeting Jesus has changed his life, and that he would rather have that than even still be a fisherman.

And Leah's happier as well. She says Jesus has given her back her husband. A few times I have noticed that she has started smiling again, even when there's nothing particular to smile about. I even heard her singing the other day.

Yes, everyone's happy. Except the wine merchants.

To tell the truth, I don't know who this Jesus is, but I do know he's managed to find the real Uncle Jake again, and I didn't think that would ever happen. I wonder what will happen if he carries on like this. I guess he'll make a lot of people very happy, but someone, odds-on a merchant or someone else whose applecart he has overturned, will most probably try to kill him!

Whole Lives – Jesus and Children

As parents and grandparents, most of us Christians recognise our responsibility to do all we can to see that the faith is passed on to our children in a way that they may claim it as their own and decide to pass it on to their children. But Jesus also turned things on their head in this area by telling us that we have much to learn from them as well.

31 Children shouting in the Temple

BACKSTORY

This event should be a constant provocation to us to consider the place and ministry of children in our midst. Children are recipients and stewards of God's gifts, just as adults are. We should make them partners with us in worship, learning and service. Reading Matthew 21:12–16 will give you the background to the story.

MONOLOGUE

So, we were all in the Temple – you know, the open bit that anyone can get in.

Really it all started before that. I don't think we even saw the first bit – at least I didn't – but I heard it. How could you *not* hear it?

You'd have to have been asleep, but you'd have woken up. Maybe if you were deaf, except my granddad's deaf but he always hears when I'm noisy. You would have had to be seriously dead to have missed it. It was just one humungous noise.

By the time I was inside, there were tables and goats and money and things everywhere. Really cool! If I'd done that, I would have been in so much trouble. My dad would have given me such a right-hander. And right in the middle of all the mess was this guy. Mum says he's a prophet. Dad says he's trouble. Grandma says he's both. I don't know about any of that stuff.

But he is cool. There he is. He's just made a serious jumble of all the market. The priests are all sulking 'cos he called them all crooks. And up come these ill guys. Half of them can't walk straight, and the other half can't see where they are walking. And I'm thinking: he's in trouble now, if this is all he's got for minders. Looks like he'd have been better off asking me and the gang for protection. How is this lot going to be of any use?

And he's not really paying attention. Just looking right at this one old boy, and touching his face. Then suddenly the old boy starts shouting. Not as much noise as before, but still enough. If I can make that much noise when I'm that old, it'll be quality.

'I can see! I can! Look, there's my wife! And there's a goat. And another one! There's goats everywhere!'

But the main man is already onto the next man. And the next. It is chaos. I reckon all heaven is breaking out. And we're all singing and everyone's dancing, specially the ones who couldn't walk straight a minute ago. One old lady kissed me! Actually, she kissed everyone. Kept saying, 'Look at the birds! Look at the sky!'

And all of a sudden the priests come over – and they're not singing. And they're not dancing. They're kind of. . . Well, Mum calls it scowling when I pull a face like that.

'That's enough! We will have order in this place. Can't you hear what these children are saying?'

But the man stops what he's doing for a minute, and says 'Yes', but he sounds pleased and tells the priests that they should be pleased. Tells them to go and read it in the book: 'You have taught children and infants to give you praise.'

So there it is. Anyone up for another of those parties?

32 The boy at the feeding of the five thousand

Listen to a child who risked all he had. We think of this as a small lunch and therefore a small risk, but then we are adults. And we live in the affluent West. The sight of your food disappearing into a crowd can be very different when you know how much it cost, when it is viewed from about four feet high, and when it is all you had to eat. Reading John 6:1–13 will give you the background to this story.

MONOLOGUE

This sounds weird, I know. But that's only 'cos it is weird.

Have you ever gone out and forgotten your lunch? Well, what I do is scrounge some off someone else. Works for me.

Usually. Only what if no one's got any? No one. You go from him to her to them and no one's got anything. I mean – think of what's left when you've eaten all your lunch!

I know – crumbs all over the floor. At least that's what Mum says, but who could eat that?

No. I mean nothing. Nothing at all. And I should know. No one's a better scrounger than me.

So there we all are – 5,000 men, plus all the women and

children. And don't go all soft on me. Some of those ankle-biters can really eat. Anyway, there we all are. The biggest spur-of-the-moment picnic this side of Jericho, only there's nothing to eat.

Everyone's come to see this Jesus, and it turns out even he's forgotten lunch. Of course I brought a bit for emergencies, but it was only a few old loaves and a couple of fish that didn't get eaten yesterday. Strictly for emergencies or extras on the way home. For more serious food you wander about eyeballing everyone's grub, choose the best and then set about charming the mum.

Only today no one's got any, and I mean no one. Think of all the people in the world. Now think of them having all the food in the world. Now imagine that my brother ate it all. Now you've got the picture of the rather sorry crowd I was hanging out with.

Now, I'm usually smart enough to make sure everyone knows not to play with my food, but this time one of Jesus' friends saw me. I had sneaked off so I could get a bite in peace, but he saw. And suddenly he says, 'You've got food!'

I know. The key word here is 'you'. That's me. I've got food. But before I could say that I'd share it any time wolves stop eating sheep, he's got it.

'Can you come with me?' he says. Can I? Can I? You've got my food. You bet I'm coming with you.

'Jesus,' he says. 'Jesus, I've met a very generous boy.' Easy. You watch where you point adjectives like generous. He goes on, 'But I don't think this meagre lunch will help.' There you go again with the adjectives. Shared among 20,000, sure it's meagre. But shared among me, it'll do just fine.

But before I get to explain my point, Jesus has the lunch

and he's praying. Then he's breaking it into bits and telling his boys to take some. And just when I'm thinking it won't go far unless I accompany it, I see four of them walking off with more than I had in the first place. Each. And he's still going for it, dishing more and more out.

And then it just got weird.

They've just finished picking up the leftovers. Twelve basketfuls. That's right. Twelve. I guess this guy doesn't waste anything – not even people like me.

33 The child in Matthew 18

BACKSTORY

The author of this book: 'When my son was about four he told me very earnestly one night as I tucked him into bed, "Dad, I've given my heart to Jesus, but it still beats really fast when I run." This monologue is dedicated to both my boys for helping me to understand the value of whole lives in the hands of our gracious God.'

Reading Matthew 18:1–4 will give you the background to this story.

MONOLOGUE

Something well cool happened today. And I mean *well* cool.

It'll probably be all over town by Saturday, but it's OK if I talk about it now. It's all about me and what happened today. I know some people won't understand but it seems to me that. . .

OK. I'm not sure I understand it, and it may not be all about me. All right, it probably wasn't all about me, but I'm the one he was looking at when he said it. So I'm going to have to explain when people ask me what he meant. It's lucky that I'm good at explaining things.

In case anyone does ask, I think I'll say something like this:

I'm just an ordinary boy. Well, *quite* ordinary. And I've never spoken to Jesus until today when I said. . . Actually, I didn't say anything today. He did all the talking. What he said to me was. . . Actually, he didn't say anything to me. Not exactly.

But he was looking at me when he said it. And he sort of pointed at me.

Anyway, what he said to me was. . . Well, he did kind of talk to me. I was playing this racing game, where everyone lines up and. . . A racing game, anyway, and I had just won the last race when Jesus called me, and I'm sure he meant me, and got me to come and stand in the middle of all his friends.

And he was saying what people should be like. And I thought he was going to say we should all be like him. Or maybe say I should be like one of his friends. But he didn't. He said they should all be like me. Well, he didn't really say 'like me'. He sort of said 'like us, like all us kids'. Really you had to be there. And it's not like everyone expected it. Everyone was like **[makes a loud sound of breathing in]** I think everyone thought he was going to say I had to be like one of his friends. But he didn't.

I suppose you want to know what he meant.

Well. . . he didn't say too much about that. What he said was that everyone had to change and become like us, 'cos we were the only ones getting in.

I don't think he meant running races and stuff. Well, he sort of did. He meant not getting bothered with grown-up stuff, like work and money and **[uses a rather disgusted voice]** 'relationships', whatever they are. But we should do really important stuff. Like breathing. And thinking. And playing. And being kind. And. . . And maybe some racing. Really anything that makes your heart beat, so you know you're alive and not just pretending.

Well, that's what I'm going to say. If anyone asks.

Healings

34 The man who was born blind

BACKSTORY

The man himself: 'You know the most common question I used to be asked? "How do blind people dream? Do you have images in your dreams, or is everything just what you hear?" The truth is, I was never sure of the answer. My dream world was much like my waking world, except that there was a heightened sense of intuition. In a dream I would always know if the other person in the dream was agreeing with me. The same way that *you* know when you see someone nodding their head. I wouldn't "see" that motion, but I would be conscious that it was happening. And you always knew where you were, by a stream or at a friend's house or wherever.'

Reading John 9 will give you the background to this story.

MONOLOGUE

I was born blind, but I had no concept of what that really meant until this morning. In fact, I didn't even know that I had been born blind at all till I was five.

When you are born without one of your senses, you will never really understand what it would have meant to have it.

Try asking a little child if he can sense things through his elbows. Tell him earnestly that everyone else can. Tell him that the rest of us can all know the contents of a scroll without hearing it read, the contents of a bag without feeling inside it, and even the contents of a meal without tasting it. Tell him we all knew he was born with a deficiency that means he can't do this, so no one talks about it much when he's around.

Probably he will just laugh and say he doesn't believe you, but even if he does believe you, he won't understand you.

Well, I was born blind. Without a sense that the rest of you take for granted. As I grew older I understood that I was missing something that for you is essential to live, and I was doomed to eke out an existence on the margins of the world, a world where all the odds were stacked against me.

I came to understand that this sense I lacked gave the rest of you an advantage. You say that it enables you not to stumble. You can tell by seeing people whether they are pleased, angry or sad. You can know if it is raining outside.

But I'm not sure that you haven't lost something too. You see, I wouldn't want that 'elbow-sense' even if there were such a thing. I like listening to people read. I like the richness of their voices, the lilt, the cadence, the accent, the way the ideas gradually unfold. I like feeling things. I like the texture and quality of things, and how they mix. The iron of an axe is harder than the handle. In the winter, that makes it colder to the touch, but if you leave an axe in the summer sun, the iron gets too hot to touch. You notice more if you experience it. I especially like tasting and eating. There is such a pleasure that comes from sweet fruit, and the taste and smell of warm bread are so comforting. No, I definitely wouldn't want that 'elbow-sense'.

If I had been born with sight, I could have been a carpenter, a farmer or a fisherman. It would have opened up a different world to me. I could have provided for my family, found a wife, raised my children. Instead, all I could ever be was a beggar sitting by the side of the road listening to people talk about me, as though having no eyes meant that I had no ears either.

But I still think that sight has made most of you poorer. Listening carefully not only to what people say, but also how they say it, seems to have made me better able than most of you to understand them. Going out without knowing that there is a gentle shower gives you the unexpected sense of rain on your skin. I love that. And stumbling teaches you not to rush, not to be proud, and allows you to experience kindness and gratefully appreciate the one who helps you to your feet. In so many ways the sight that empowers you in this world and wouldn't admit me has made you too rushed – even at times too impatient or too proud – to notice, let alone value, what I notice.

But being blind has robbed me. I will never know what it is to race around with childhood friends, enjoy an admiring look from one of the girls or have so many of the growing-up experiences that I've heard others talking about.

But I would have swapped them all anyway for what just happened to me this morning.

I was simply sitting by the road as normal, listening as the world went past, when some Galileans stopped near me to talk. I could tell they were Galileans from their accents. They were talking about me, as it happens; the same old mistake of thinking that blind people are deaf. It might even have been interesting if they hadn't been so insensitive as to talk right over my head.

One was saying, 'Of course all sickness is the result of sin.' Another disagreed. 'Whose sin?' he said. 'Whose sin? Are you really saying that all people who are lame, deaf or blind are worse than the rest of us?' And yet another added, 'Anyway, he's sat here for years. He's always here. I heard that he was born blind.' Another voice: 'I suppose it might be his parents. Is it not written that the Lord is a jealous God, punishing the children for the sins of the fathers?'

I wanted to ask, 'And whose fault is it that you were all born terminally stupid?', but I don't think they would have heard me even if I had spoken.

In the end a rabbi must have been passing, and one of them called to him, 'Rabbi, who sinned, this man or his parents, that he was born blind?' But nothing could have prepared me for the reply.

To start with, there was the rabbi's voice. I'd never heard anyone sound so authoritative and yet so concerned at the same time. This was not the voice of a legalistic, self-assured pedant, but one with the kind of authority that comes from experience, although I can't think of any experience under heaven that could make a man know what he knew.

'Neither,' he said. 'This precious one has been set aside by God so his life could be a demonstration of God's goodness.'

I wanted to say, 'Well, he might have asked first', but the words died on my lips as I felt him touch my eyes. He had placed some mud on them, which he now said I should wash off at the nearest well. Again, I wanted to say, '*You* go and get the water. You made the mud.' But I felt what I can only describe as a hand resting on my heart, checking the scorn that I had quietly nurtured over the years; so I asked a passer-by to lead me to the well. By the time I got there most of the mud had been washed off by tears.

I wouldn't have admitted it, even to myself, but I had accumulated years of disappointment, cynicism and even resentment. Life seemed to have set me apart from people who could realistically expect to be able to gain reasonable returns for their endeavours. But when that rabbi talked of me being set aside by God, my disdain for others began to unravel like a garment that has been caught on a nail.

When I washed my eyes, what really washed off was the mud that I felt life had thrown at me. And then I stepped into another world, one of light. I can see. I understand what you were all saying all these years. No one told me the world was so beautiful! No one said it had so much rich variety. The only thing that I realise hasn't changed as I watch the doctors of the law struggling to come to terms with the life-affirming miracle that has just happened to me is that there are still some tragic individuals who appear to have been born terminally stupid.

35 The paralysed man

BACKSTORY

His wife: 'You might think that experiences like my husband's accident would give rise to some kind of brutal solidarity with those who have received the vicious capriciousness that life can mete out. But not in his case. He just cut everyone off. His life became an act of hubris, a manoeuvre of defiance. And all I could do was watch. Thank God for friends who loved him.'

Reading Mark 2:1–12 will give you the background to this story.

MONOLOGUE

So what?

That was my first thought. So what?

Jesus is at home. So what?

I've never been one for rabbis. Holy Joes, mostly. And I had no reason to believe this one would be any different. Patronising, condescending and so holy that you just know it isn't real.

And don't go thinking that it's just bitterness talking. I was like this before the accident. . . All the accident did was to confirm what I always used to say: 'If you really want to make God laugh, tell him your plans.' And I had so many plans – until that wally with his plough did for my legs. I wasn't bitter against him. I didn't resent him for being such an airhead that he didn't watch where he was going. I was a very fair, even-handed man. I had the same disdain for everyone.

I had been on my way to the top. Not that I was arrogant or anything like that. I just reckoned that I was better than pretty much all of the people I knew. I was going to be richer, more powerful, and have more influence than all of them put together. Sure I would help orphaned kids and widows; just as long as everyone knew that I was only doing it 'cos I was stinking rich.

All that came to an end the day I walked across my field to talk to my ploughman. That was in the days when I had a ploughman, and some fields for him to plough. That was before I slipped and he decided to plough me.

It's amazing how many people want to help, even though most of them end up helping themselves to your business. I lost everything when I lost control of my legs. Everything. All I could do was sit and stare at the walls. Nothing to do. No friends to talk to. Just me and four walls.

And to cap it all, one day I get kidnapped. Kidnapped, I say. Taken by four men from the village, who seemed determined to be what they regarded as 'friendly'; taken against my better judgement to see this Jesus. 'He's home for a bit. This could be the only chance we'll have to get you to see him. We've thought it all through. If we get you to lie on this stretcher that we've knocked up, we can bring you to the house where he is in under an hour.' Only they hadn't quite thought it *all* through. They had overlooked a couple of minor details.

One, I didn't want to go. They didn't seem too worried by

that. Just rolled me onto the stretcher and off we went. When you can't move your legs, you're kind of at the mercy of well-meaning, friendly people, even if you haven't seen them in over three months.

Two – well, that was a little more tricky. One very bumpy hour later we arrived at the house only to find we couldn't get in. Couldn't even get near. You've never seen anything like it! Wall-to-wall people, and after that more people. People were blocking up the door, blocking up every window and blocking most of the street.

'OK, guys,' I said. 'You've had your bit of fun. Now for pity's sake, can we please go home?'

But they weren't having any of it. 'Quit now? When we're this close? You never used to be a quitter.' And before I could say, 'Give it up, you numbskulls! We're going home', they had taken me round the back, up the stairs, onto the roof, and had started to break through.

Terrific. Breaking and entering. They were doing the breaking, and I was doing the entering, lowered down through the roof. I was just reaching for the appropriate invective when I found myself face to face with the rabbi.

There was a momentary silence, and then he looked up at the guys who had broken the roof and laughed. He almost seemed to find the whole thing entertaining.

Then he looked at me, but this time he wasn't laughing. 'Son,' he said (though he can't have been much older than me), 'your sins are forgiven.'

I was just about to say 'What sins?' when my mind seemed to fill with pictures and snatches of conversation. I could see my two brothers and hear myself telling them, 'It didn't happen to you. It happened to me. And I don't need your help and I don't need you!'

And then I saw the people who had cheated me out of my business and remembered how I had wished them all dead.

And now the pictures came so fast. My mother, my wife, my kids, all surrounded by the sound of my voice being unbiddable, unkind, ungrateful.

I guess I did need forgiving. Needed cleaning up. Needed redirecting. Going to the top isn't all it's cracked up to be, not if you have to climb over everyone in the way. And especially not if you make everyone else's life a misery when you don't make it, whatever the reason.

It never occurred to me to doubt him. I could tell from his voice and the look on his face that the way I'd behaved had been an issue for him. And I knew at that moment that he had decided to forgive me for it.

Then the sound of the rabbi's voice brought me back to the room. He sounded impatient, talking to the scribes who were there.

His eyes were full of a silent rage. 'Which is easier? To say his sins are forgiven or to actually tell him to walk? But in order to show you that I have the authority to forgive sins. . .' and he turned to me. 'You can get up now.'

It never occurred to me to doubt him then, either. 'You can take your stretcher and go home.' I stood up. Everyone gasped. I gathered up my stuff. Everyone made room for me as I walked out. He looked up at the hole in the roof and my four friends. And he smiled.

36 Bartimaeus

BACKSTORY

Bartimaeus: 'The times I have had to say, "I'm blind, not deaf. Not paralysed. Not dead. And it's supposed to be me that can't see you, not the other way round." It can be an effort to get noticed when you can't see. But sometimes you've just got to yell. This time it was different, though. I wasn't yelling so that my hearers would get it into their skulls. I was yelling so that my hearers would know I meant business. Sometimes I think God only deals with the desperate.'

Reading Mark 10:46–52 will give you the background to this story.

MONOLOGUE

Being blind means you have to try harder. Just to survive. Just to eat. If I want to go somewhere on the day that I want, rather than having to go on the end of someone's priorities, I have to try harder. If I want to go further than just stepping outside, I will need help.

Why would you want to help me?

My parents died years ago. They couldn't have children after me, so I've no brothers or sisters. I never married.

There was going to be time. But there wasn't. I went blind. Only took a few months.

I couldn't weave any more like my father. But it was all I knew. What else could I do? I couldn't work fishing. I'd have been no use tending flocks.

All I could do was beg. I suppose I could have been a tax collector. I guess that's a bit like being a beggar – you get people to give you money that you haven't worked for. Only, tax collectors have two advantages over beggars. They have soldiers to back them up, and they have no conscience to trip them up.

'You can't afford your taxes this month? It's been a poor month's fishing? Don't worry! I'll tell you what we will do. Just give it to me when you can. No rush. Now, which finger should I get the big man over there to break in the meantime?'

You may get less money if you have to ask nicely, but you get to keep hold of your soul.

The doctors said there was something wrong with my eyes. Incredible. They worked that out all by themselves, just after I told them I couldn't see. I suppose I could have been a doctor, maybe a specialist. Specialising in the stunningly obvious.

But then again, maybe not.

So, having reviewed all my options, I ended up being a beggar. No ordinary beggar, I like to think. To persuade people to give you money, when you obviously can't give them anything back, takes talent. Of course it helps that so many people remember my father, Timaeus the weaver. They still think of me as Timaeus's lad, even though he passed on 20 long years ago.

'Look, Joanna! Isn't that Timaeus's lad? You remember, he used to be such a tall young man.'

Used to be? Hello?

Try it for yourself sometime. Just wander through the market, not talking but just listening. People say some really mind-numbing things sometimes. Actually a lot of the time.

Course, it helps that I'm blind. People often treat you as though you can't hear when you can't see, as though going blind makes you deaf. Irritating, but you do get to hear some stuff.

But I don't think I've ever heard anyone say that going blind makes you shorter before.

I didn't *used to be* a tall young man. I'm *still* a tall young man. I'm just sitting down.

Anyhow, all this is way off the point. You've probably heard of that healer from Nazareth. Causing quite a stir. Well, he was here last week. In Jericho. I couldn't get to him. Crowd was too big. Remember me saying that being blind means you have to try harder? Well, I got someone to take me to the road I reckoned he would leave by.

Sat there on my own for days. Just beginning to think I may have picked the wrong road when suddenly loads of people turned up. And in less than an hour, I could hear them all saying, 'Look – here he comes!'

Well, that was my cue. I knew I was only going to get one go at this, so I yelled with all my voice, 'Jesus! Have mercy on me!' And I kept on yelling. I suppose there's always a few who think the world is only there for their personal convenience. One woman got quite agitated; told me to shut up. Always inconvenient when someone else's problem disturbs your peace. But this might have been my only chance. So I ignored her. 'Jesus! Have mercy on me!' I don't really know what I expected to happen. Of course I'd heard the stories. That's why I was there. And suddenly it went quiet, and someone said, 'Looks like your lucky day. He said to take you into the road to see him.' Any other day I would have pointed out that luck had nothing to do with it. I had missed three good begging days just waiting for this, but it no longer seemed to matter. The cynicism left me. Just as well. The next minute Jesus was asking me, 'What do you want me to do for you?'

And I could hear soul in his voice. He cared how I answered. I actually think he was just willing me to ask the right thing, so I took everything in me and put it all into one request, 'Lord, I want to regain my sight!'

I know it sounds unlikely now, even ridiculous, but it was all I could think about. In that question he seemed to be asking me everything, understanding my whole life. And in that answer I told him it all. Told him everything I dreaded and everything I hoped for. I staked it all on that appeal. It had my whole life in it, and a silent pledge of the rest of my life. I meant it like nothing I had ever told anyone before.

And the words of his reply, 'Receive your sight; your faith has saved you and made you well', contained the whole world for me. Yes, with those words he restored my sight, but, if you can understand, it was the least thing he gave me that day. He confirmed his ownership of my life. Nothing bad can ever happen in my life ever again, because I don't have one. I gave it to him.

Drinking the Cup – Stories of Martyrdom

37 Stephen

BACKSTORY

When we read about Jesus in heaven as he is now, we get a picture of him being seated on his throne. But we are told that he stood to welcome Stephen into heaven. Such is Christ's esteem for those who lay down their lives for him. In considering their lives, we tread on holy ground. Reading Acts 6:1–15, 7:54–60 will give you the background to this story.

MONOLOGUE

[Rising from his knees, visibly shaken]

I have just been to look at my three little girls, all asleep. All tangled up together on the mattress. How they don't wake each other up all night I'll never know. But they don't. Just looking at them all lying there makes you realise that even with their childish spats, they really do love each other.

A few weeks ago I lost my patience over an uncharacteristic piece of pettiness. I had to tell them off for squabbling over some simple task that I had asked them to do for their mother. 'Look, I don't care if you do this bit and she does that bit, or if you all work together. I just want you to do the job without arguing or complaining.' And in that moment, I am sure I heard God laughing, as though he was saying, 'Now you know what it feels like!' So it came as no surprise to me when Simon Peter asked me to take responsibility for a work ensuring that both the Hebraic and the Grecian widows were equally cared and provided for.

There have been some wrangles over whether each part of the community was being treated fairly, and I know that this was troubling the apostles. I know Peter was particularly concerned about making sure that the church was always fair. In the end he asked the community to identify some trustworthy individuals to bring some order to this sorry state of affairs. I was really honoured that people saw me in this way.

But that's not why I have just been over to look at the girls. I wanted to give each one a kiss, and whisper prayers over them while they slept. The prophets tell us, 'Arise, cry out in the night; pour out your heart like water in the presence of the Lord. Lift up your hands to him for the lives of your children', and oftentimes I pray for them in this way.

But tonight felt different. It was as though God was asking me, 'Do you trust me with them? Do you believe I will do right by them, even if you aren't able to be there for them?' It was harder to say yes to that than I would readily admit. They are my little angels. I know their future depends on him, and not on me. But it is not easy to imagine not being there for them.

Going back to our bed, I felt God ask me the same about Lois. I know she is a woman of God. I know her whole life is shot through with love for Christ. But for the ten years that she has been my wife I have been her companion, provider and protector. We came to faith in Christ together.

We were baptised together. I have never truly asked myself that question. Do I trust God for her? In his order of things, she is his daughter before she is my wife. And I know that she would say the same. But this question suddenly seemed so pressing, so immediate.

And suddenly God turned me to a bigger picture. I saw the city of Jerusalem as if I were watching it from the sky. I saw tendrils of fire suddenly shooting out into the surrounding country. We have always said that the gospel was for Jerusalem, Judea and the ends of the earth. The gospel is my passion. I remember the story that Andrew tells of how, when he first met the Lord, he ran to find his brother Simon. Simon hadn't really wanted to know, but Andrew knew that if Simon saw Jesus for himself, then he would believe. I know there are those who are yet strangers, even hostile, to our faith, but God will touch them. Even one with a ministry as great as Simon Peter's can be brought to faith by the faith of another. Lois and I have always said that if God sent us, we would go, even to the ends of the earth, whatever the cost. But now it all seems very imminent.

It's like Jesus said, 'Zeal for your house has consumed me.' A fierce flame is a mesmerising thing to watch. But am I ready to be caught up in such a consuming fire? I know now that the fire in Jerusalem will spread, and that it will spread soon. And any flame in the fire can burn brightly, but sometimes only for a short time.

For days now God has been asking me if I am willing for such a life. To be more concerned about the brightness of my flame than about how long it lasts. It's easy to say yes glibly, but this question has been exercising my heart for weeks. Am I ready to be consumed in the great inferno of the gospel? Does my love for Jesus eclipse all other loves?

In truth, I am genuinely not sure what my answer to that question has ever been. But today, God has given me the grace to say yes.

Note

In June 1950 Jim Elliot, a young graduate from a Christian college, went to a summer language school where he met a former missionary to the Quichua Indians of Ecuador and first heard of the remote and much-feared Huaorani tribe in that country. His response was immediately to ask God if he should go to this tribe with the gospel. After a ten-day period of prayer for guidance, Jim wrote to another missionary in Ecuador offering to come and help. He first went there late in 1951.

On Sunday, 8 January 1956 Jim was with some friends in the region of the Huaorani. These men radioed their wives at 12:30 p.m. saying that they expected to meet some of the Huaorani that afternoon and that they would radio again at 4:30 p.m. They never got to make that second call. A few days later, Jim Elliot's body was found downstream with three others. They had been killed with wooden lances and machetes. The deaths of these men were reported world-wide, and they were regarded by many as twentieth-century martyrs. Jim's wife, Elisabeth, later returned to Shandia and resumed the work of her husband. Along with another lady who was also widowed in the 1956 incident, she went to live with the Huaorani group in 1959.

Listen to Jim Elliot's words:

'Am I ignitable?' I mean, right away, doesn't that grab you? When was the last time you even thought to ask God that question? 'Oh God, am I ignitable? God, deliver me from the dread asbestos of other things. Saturate me with the oil of the Spirit, that I might be a flame. But flame is transient, often short-lived. Canst thou bear this, my soul? Short life? In me there dwells the spirit of the great short-lived, whose zeal for God's house consumed him. Make me thy fuel, flame of God. He is no fool who gives what he cannot keep to gain what he cannot lose.'

38 John the Baptist's jailer

BACKSTORY

One of John's disciples: 'I've never wanted to laugh and cry at the same time before. Hearing that John had laid down his life for Jesus was the toughest news I'd ever heard. Going to collect and bury his body was the toughest thing I had ever done. I once heard Jesus ask those of us who followed John, "What did you go out into the desert to see?" and answer, "I tell you, he was more than a prophet." And so he was. There was so much to love in that man. Telling Jesus the news will be the toughest thing of all.'

Reading Matthew 14:1–12 will give you the background to this story.

MONOLOGUE

This job is worthless, total rubbish. I hate it.

When I joined up I had dreams of one day being selected for the elite, the Praetorian Guard, not overseeing slaves in a filthy fleapit of a Jewish prison. And for what? To help Herod, the local self-important lackey for Rome, keep order in this wretched corner of the world.

I had dreams of glory, returning from mighty conquests, heralded as one of Rome's heroes. Instead I get this: to help this puppet king maintain order. Well, it's not why I joined.

Everyone's bored. There is nothing to do. I mean nothing. These people argue incessantly. Herod seems gripped by a burning ambition to remain king over the most quarrelsome bunch of fishermen and shepherds who live in Rome's most dismal province. There's not many of us Romans here, and there is nothing to do.

Some of the lads get their kicks by watching people suffer. After all, the prisoners aren't Roman citizens, and Herod doesn't seem to care what we do, and sometimes I hear screams coming from the cells, which means that one of our boys is kicking the life out of one of the scum. I can't be bothered. Like I said, it's not why I joined.

The first interesting thing happened here when they brought in a preacher. Apparently he insulted Herod's wife, Herodias – not that that's anything to write home about. I don't think anyone actually likes her. She's a scheming, manipulative harpy who's slept her way to the top. Mind you, she is a stunner.

Anyhow, the mistake this preacher made was to say it in public. Well, Herod couldn't exactly ignore that, so he had him brought in, but he couldn't make up his mind what to do with him. He even had him brought up out of the cells just to talk to him. I could hardly believe it, first time he did it. He didn't have him beaten. He didn't even yell. They just talked. Well, Herodias was furious. Stormed around for days, with a face so evil I reckon she could've killed one of Hannibal's elephants just by looking at it.

But Herod kept on doing it. In the end I went to have a look at him in the cells. When I thought none of the lads were around I even went in to talk to him a few times. It isn't easy to talk down there. It stinks of sweat and blood and fear, and it's as hot as Hades, but listening to him was actually worth it, in a strange kind of way.

I can't say what it was, but something about him made me keep going back. He could create an aura as stern as my father, as kindly as my granddad and as mysterious as the oracle at Delphi. I really couldn't figure him out.

And he kept on about this character Jesus. I'd never heard of him, but John spoke of little else. Said he'd spent his whole life, 30 years, just waiting for him. Said he was going to save the world. Said he would eradicate all evil. When *I* repeat it, it sounds ridiculous, but when *he* said it I almost believed it.

One time I tried to make him understand how much danger he was really in, but he just laughed. Kept saying *I* was in much more danger than him; that a crisis was coming to the world that would force everyone to choose, not between what we believe is right and wrong, but between living for his Jesus or living for ourselves. He kept calling this Jesus the world's rightful king.

Now, I've heard that Herod's father, Herod the Great, once put all the baby boys in an entire town to death just because someone said that the next king would be born in that town. And actually that could be true. His obsessiveness was legendary. I told John that it wasn't safe to say such things, but again he just laughed.

I don't know why, but I just haven't been able to put him out of my mind. Would you believe that he had only met this Jesus guy once, and only for less than an hour? Yet when he spoke of him, his face shone. His voice filled with passion and his eyes frequently watered up.

I warned him that he could even be killed here, right in this cell, but he seemed genuinely unconcerned. He said that while he lived he would serve this Jesus. He even said once that his God had brought me here, to Israel, to this very cell, not to do anything for him but just to hear about his Jesus.

Only once did I really get through to him. Herodias was in one of her rages and said that if Herod wouldn't do it, then she was going to come down here to John's cell and kill him herself. I don't believe that she would risk dirtying her clothes, but it showed how much she hated him. I told John, and for once he looked serious. He said he believed that she might kill him one day. He said that he didn't expect to leave the cells as a free man. He didn't really expect to get out alive.

And then this morning, I arrive to hear talk all over the palace. This time she's really done it – tricked Herod into promising her daughter anything for the way she danced, and then told her to ask for John's head. And, true to form, Herod behaved like the cowardly, dirty old man he really is, and sent a guard to chop it off.

I've just been in John's cell. His headless, lifeless body is lying on the floor. I don't know if this Jesus he kept on about was really worth it. All I know is that a very brave man thought he was.

39 James, the brother of John

A guard: 'You definitely do some unsocial hours in this job. We had to pick this guy up early this morning. "Get him while he's at home in bed," they told us. But in a strange way he almost seemed to be expecting us. Anyhow, I don't think he'll still be here by supper. I think Herod's going to make an example of this one.'

Reading Matthew 20:20–23 and then Acts 12:1–2 will give you the background to this story.

MONOLOGUE

I think this might be it.

The guard who brought me in shoved me in the cell by the door, saying, 'You can get in there. We usually put prisoners somewhere worse, to break them, make them more manageable, but you aren't going to be lucky enough to need that.' And he walked away, laughing.

It's hard to believe that they can have anywhere worse than this. It's dark; it's hot; it's damp. It smells of blood and despair. I'm sure that there are rats. I heard one scurry through just now.

Something like this was always in the offing with a man

like Herod on the throne. His grandfather was a mad old tyrant. He once killed an entire village full of children in an unsuccessful bid to kill Jesus as an infant. One of his uncles killed John the Baptist and then the Christ himself. So it was always on the horizon that this one would want to kill some of us. It's like Jesus said, 'If they hate you, keep in mind that they hated me first.'

I was picked up by Herod's men this morning.

It's so hot in here. There's no air. I can hear running water outside. What I wouldn't give for a drink. . . I heard one guard tell another outside the cell, 'No water for that one. Why waste it? He's not going to need it.' I think he meant me.

Jesus himself specifically told me to expect to drink from his cup, to suffer in his name. He said the same to John and later said the same to Peter, but he also said to him that he would not drink from this cup until he was old. 'When you are old, someone else will dress you and lead you where you do not want to go.' Those were his very words. 'When you are old. . .' So Herod can't have picked up all of us. I wonder if I'm the only one.

I have never expected to live that long, never thought of having an old age, but now it comes apace.

I can still remember meeting Jesus for the first time. On the shore of the lake. He had been using Simon Peter's boat from which to address the crowd. Struck me as odd. They didn't really know each other, and Peter rarely lent anyone his stuff. Still, it was morning. We had done with it for the day. And everyone was tired after a completely fruitless night, having worked a whole eight hours and not caught a thing. Grafted all out and felt all in. And all of a sudden Jesus starts telling us what to do: 'Put out into deeper water, and let down the nets for a catch.'

Now, Peter was an obdurate man. I don't think, up to that point, I had ever seen him do anything if it wasn't his own idea. So, when he merely muttered the mildest of protests before doing what Jesus had said, it felt like a miracle. When the nets actually filled with fish, then I knew we had just crossed into the unknown. When Peter knelt at Jesus' feet, my life changed for ever. As he often did, he said what all of us were feeling: 'There must be some mistake. We're just ordinary fishermen, not ready for heaven to invade our lives, and I am certainly not a holy man.' But even as I heard him speak, I knew it was too late. I was already enthralled, captivated by Jesus. I felt as though I had just been born into another world – one where very little of what I thought I knew was right.

I still am captivated by him. The last time I got to sit at his feet, he had just given all of us breakfast on the shore of the lake. But more than that, he had given us one more mystery. I thought that I now knew how it was. God now held centre stage for me. He held supremacy. I would live my life at his beck and call. In three years, I told my friends, Jesus had shown me everything in a different light.

But even that wasn't quite true. Death still seemed fairly certain. In that last week Jesus had received a beating from which he never would have recovered. But to speed up his death they went on to crucify him, killing him by overpowering his ability even to breathe. And then, just to make absolutely sure, they stabbed him. And three days later here he was, serving breakfast.

The last vestiges of my old life left me that day. He really was all there was to life. It was the most awesome experience: a handful of disparate, rough and ready young men sitting on the beach with Jesus, bound together by admiration for him, discovering that none of the usual laws of earth applied to a man who could get over death like the rest of us get over a bad dream. This was a real new birth.

I have loved him since that first day I met him on that shore. And so, once again I sit by the shore, another shore, an eternal shore. In a few hours angry men will parade me as their prisoner and then execute me. But I will leave this shore for the other side, the real side, where everything is so much more solid than this world of mists and shadows which I am in now.

God, help me to show everyone what I learned that day. Death holds no fear. I have often yearned to sit at his feet again. When you follow the only man who has taken death at its height and made nothing of it, death holds no fear. In an hour or two, I will be sitting at his feet again.

*Unexpected Endings – Accounts of the
Dead Brought to Life*

40 Jairus

BACKSTORY

Jairus is called a 'ruler of the synagogue' in Mark 5:22. This means he was the leader of a team of elders who had charge of the synagogue. This team would have worked as a deliberative body, but at the same time Jairus had final responsibility for the maintenance of good order in the synagogue and the orthodoxy of its members. It would not have been a full-time role. He would have had disciplinary power, in that he was authorised to reprimand, and even to excommunicate, people of whose actions he disapproved. You often see rulers using this power against Jesus and his followers, but here Jairus is caught in a dilemma. Should he follow conventional orthodoxy? Or should he follow his heart and trust the healer? Reading Luke 8:40–56 will give you the background to this story.

MONOLOGUE

Today started gracelessly. No one likes bad news. Yet the chain of events today has exceeded anything I have ever experienced.

I am a farmer. Last night we had a dreadful thunderstorm, and this morning many of our crops have been damaged. Nathan, a young apprentice who works with me, says that our fields are waterlogged, and one of our oxen seems to have become so bothered by the noise and the lightning that it broke down the fence and escaped.

I never got the chance to ask if the other livestock were all right before my eldest girl got up. I think the noise woke her. Today was her twelfth birthday. She would probably have offered to get everyone a drink. She's always been like that, eager to help. But instead, as soon as she stood, she fell, overcome with sickness. Any parent will know what I mean when I say I knew something was wrong, so wrong. It was out of the ordinary, no run-of-the-mill queasiness, but violent trauma. She complained last night of feeling ill, but my wife put it down to the heat. Yesterday was sultry, and she had run around a lot. Now I regret not paying this whole matter much more attention.

Then I did something that I have rarely done before. I asked Nathan to leave and attend to the problems on the farm without me.

She got worse. I had never seen her so distressed. I am no physician, and although we sent for one, no one came. And she continued to lose ground. Something like this happens and you suddenly feel vulnerable, sensing how fragile life can be. She only turned twelve today. A life shouldn't end at twelve, not when so much of it has yet to be lived.

I am a shepherd of the people in this town, asked by the town elders to serve as ruler of the synagogue. I know that God's sheep can fall prey to life's hardships. I have stood with many at times of trial or crisis but never had my own house plundered in this way before. There is no value in asking questions that can't be answered, but such hardship as this is painful – merciless, inflexible. She had so much life even yesterday, and I have had to watch it drain from her so fast today, feeling so powerless.

I am quite a private man, but, since the news got out, people have been arriving all day – some to offer help, which was appreciated, some to commiserate, which was hard, and some because they are drawn by any unfortunate predicament as a moth is drawn to a flame. One told me that a healer was in town. I naturally avoid such types – usually self-seeking charlatans, the worst kind of showmen. I went only because I had no choice. There was no one else to help, and no time.

It took half an hour to reach him – it seemed an age. When I found him, he was surrounded by a larger crowd than I had ever seen, heaving and jostling. Something about him seemed to exude hope. Suddenly I knew it. I must push through the crowd, must reach him. Doing this brought home to me my own desperation, made me tearful, caused me to fall at his feet and beg, oblivious to who was there or what they thought. He made as if to come with me, then suddenly called out, 'Who touched me?'

I hadn't seen it before, but now I realised that some near him knew him. One of them said, 'Master, the people are crowding and pressing against you. What do you mean, "Who touched me?"? There are hundreds.'

But the healer replied, 'Someone touched me; I felt power go out from me.' I didn't know how to feel. Was this showmanship? But such types rarely allow associates to question them like that, fearful of losing the crowd's attention. It was certainly unwelcome to me. My girl was the only one in my soul at that moment; everything else was an uninvited distraction.

No one answered him, but he persisted. Finally, a woman spoke. She looked shaken that he knew what she had done. For my part, I still don't understand what she had done. I didn't hear what she said, wasn't listening, only quietly weeping for my girl. Then came the blow. A servant of mine had reached us and spoke quietly. 'I'm sorry.' He said more, most of which I didn't hear. But through the blur I caught the words 'She's dead'. I was unprepared. I turned to walk. When you have to catch an animal, it struggles and kicks till you overpower it. I wanted to struggle and kick, but the words overpowered me, brought me down with a single blow. I stopped weeping. I felt that I had stopped living.

Then the healer caught my arm. He had such a good voice. 'Don't be afraid. Let's go to your house.' And I trusted him. With the only part of me left that could feel anything, I trusted him.

As we neared the house, still thronged by people, suddenly there appeared still more people, crying and wailing, surrounding us. And then he spoke again: 'This is not needed. Return to your homes.' Mocking laughter ensued, but again he persisted. I don't know how he did it, but soon I was in the house, and it was just me, my wife, the healer and three of his friends. And there she was, still and colourless, lifeless and joyless. A body – but no longer my girl. She had gone, left behind her form, but gone for all that.

He took her hand. At that moment some inexplicable hope gripped me. 'Little girl, I say to you, get up.' At that moment I hoped. Against all despair, even against all hope, I hoped. If the time I spent looking for him seemed like an age, this was more like eternity. Time seemed to freeze. The people and events surrounding me began to fade. I could only see my girl. And then she sneezed. And shook herself. And sat up. And filled the room with one of her precious smiles.

That man didn't just restore her life. He held it, as he now holds mine. I found out later his name is Jesus.

41 The widow of Nain

Jesus repeated the importance of supporting widows throughout his ministry. The Gospel of Luke alone contains six references to widows: Luke 2:36, 4:26, 7:11, 18:1, 20:47 and 21:1. His concern for widows was just one of the ways in which his whole treatment of women was radical. (He talked to women, even foreign women or others who were ritually impure. He taught women about the ways of God and even accepted them into his inner circle of friends. He appeared first to a woman after his resurrection.) When Jesus met this widow from Nain who had just lost her son, we are told that 'his heart went out to her'. And the rest, as they say, is history. Reading Luke 7:11–17 will give you the background to this story.

MONOLOGUE

I still can't get used to it. I don't think I'll ever get used to it.

Only last week, he seemed so. . . he seemed so alive! Well, he was. And now he's dead. It's not just the sudden nature of it, not even the final nature of it. It's just the capricious, random nature of it that hangs all of your feelings out to dry.

Why? There isn't anyone to be angry with. It was just an accident. If he had been a minute earlier, if he had walked a little faster, if the brakes on the cart had worked a little better, if he hadn't stopped earlier to help a child who had got separated in the crowd from his mum, if the cart had crashed into someone other than him. . . He helps a little boy who has lost his mother, and now I've lost my son.

I want to say people shouldn't leave carts at the top of hills. I want to say people should take more care when making and using brakes. I don't even know whether it was someone else's son releasing the cart for a laugh. I want to say people in market crowds should pay more attention when someone calls 'Look out!' But it's really no one's fault.

Someone could have pushed him out of the way. If they had, he would have laughed and never really thought about how much danger he missed that day.

He was always laughing. Everything was a reason for laughing. Bad weather just made him laugh at us for thinking it inconvenient. The antics of the children in the village always made him laugh. The goat that we keep in the yard always made him laugh, although I was constantly telling him not to tease it.

He was always happy. His work made him happy. The thought of his impending marriage had made him very happy. He even used to say that I had made him happy.

My friend says that while I keep these memories of him alive in my heart, in a way it keeps him alive. He was a kind, caring, young man. He was thoughtful and curious, constantly asking questions.

But it doesn't change the fact that he's dead. Memories won't play with the village children. They won't take Leah, his sweetheart, on moonlit strolls. They won't make me a grandmother, or look after me when I'm old.

Maybe in time I will find a certain comfort in them. But now all they do is confound my thinking, scuttle my feelings and muddy my prayers.

I can't decide whether to thank God that I had him, that I knew him for all the years he was here, or whether to just fade away into my unanswered questions and unabated grief. He was my pride and my joy, the source of my identity with the other mothers of the town, the one person in whose memories I thought I might live after I'm gone.

But now he's dead, and I don't know where I am going to find anything else to care about.

Now all the villagers have gathered to start the procession, to carry him out of my house, out of the village and out of my life. I never wondered about how I would feel when this day came because I never thought about such a thing at all, but all I want to do is wail. I am content to allow someone else to lead me. I can't see through my tears anyway.

[Pause]

Why have we stopped? Who is that standing in the way?

[Repeating Jesus' words to her:] Don't cry? Why not? What else is there to do? Why touch him? What. . . ?
    Matthew! How. . . ?

[Kneels down] Master.

[Pause – moves to a different part of the stage]

So now everyone's gone. Left me on my own. But I don't mind. There's been a terrific hullabaloo here all afternoon. My head is spinning. Matthew is alive.

Now he's gone off round the village with Leah in the vain hope of finding someone who hasn't already heard what's happened. But he'll be back.

He'll be back. How can it be? This morning I had lost him for ever. And now? Now I can say, nonchalantly, 'He'll be back.' I'm still not sure who it was that did this, still less how it happened. How can anyone graciously, casually and devastatingly turn the world on its head? I'd like to find the man, although just saying 'thank you' seems inadequate.

I still can't get used to it. I don't think I'll ever get used to it.

42 One of the witnesses before he talked to the Pharisees

BACKSTORY

We are told of some who went to the Pharisees and told them what Jesus had done. Other scriptures show us just how aggressive the Pharisees could be when told something they didn't want to hear (see John 9:16–23). Reading John 11:45–48 will give you the background to this story.

MONOLOGUE

I'm going to face some tough questioning later today. I suppose it would be quite unrealistic to hope they haven't heard what happened. It's possible that they haven't heard that I was there.

Possible, I suppose. But if I'm honest, not that likely. I was Lazarus's friend. No, that's wrong. I *am* Lazarus's friend.

Still can't get used to that. A few days gone by, and I was just getting used to referring to him in the past tense when all of a sudden it's present tense again. I *am* Lazarus's friend. At least I hope I am. And I hope I still will be after tomorrow.

They can't expect me to say any different from what I saw. And that was very straightforward, although it sounds seriously odd. But if I stick to the undisputed facts, what can they do to me?

Lazarus died. Now that's an uncontested fact. We buried him. Fact number two.

So far, so good. He dies. We bury him. It's sad, but it's not remarkable. Not out of the ordinary. In fact, it's very ordinary. There's a whole variety of reasons why you can't say that he wasn't dead, but the chief reason why you can't say he wasn't dead is that he was.

Everyone knows it. The whole village came to his funeral. Mary was there. Martha was there. All his friends were there. The only person who wasn't there, but might reasonably have been expected to be there, was Jesus. After all, they were quite close. Oops, I did it again! They *are* quite close. I suppose you could also have said that they *were* quite close, except you could only have said that when Lazarus was dead. But now he's better, they *are* quite close again.

Actually they *are* probably even better friends than they *were*. After all, it's not every day that someone helps you get better after you've died, now is it? And that's what happened, and that's fact number three.

Jesus wasn't there at first. Several people commented on that. And then, all of a sudden, there he was. Someone must have told Mary, 'cos she suddenly disappeared off and came back with Jesus. And they talked for a short time, and then Jesus set off in the direction of the tomb.

Then he did a seriously odd thing. He got some of the men to open the tomb. I couldn't believe it. I would never do anything that odd.

And then he prayed an even odder prayer. He said, 'Father, I thank you that you have heard me. I know you always hear me, but I said this so everyone else could hear it.' I've certainly never prayed anything that odd.

And then the oddest thing yet. He shouted at Lazarus to come out of the tomb. Now you wouldn't expect Lazarus to hear him, on account of him being dead and all. But he did. Out he came, all wrapped up as if he was still dead. And Jesus didn't bat an eyelid, just said 'Someone help him out of all that stuff.'

And that's the problem. Not a problem for Lazarus, obviously. But definitely a problem for me. Doing things that are odd isn't a crime, but they aren't going to like it. Already, the ones in the Council of Israel that have heard about it are not happy.

I overheard some of them talking. One of them said, 'What are we accomplishing? Here is this man performing many miraculous signs. If we let him go on like this, everyone will believe in him, and you know what that means!'

And of course he was right. What are they accomplishing? Not a lot. In fact, if the truth be told, I don't think they ever have done. If you ask me (which, I know, no one actually is), most of the time the Council is a talking-shop.

I know they couch their opposition to him in nice, important-sounding, theological terms, but if you ask me it's just jealousy. He's popular; they're not. He is certainly accomplishing loads; they're not. He's just brought a dead man back from the grave, and most of this lot look like they'd struggle to bring a dead chicken back from the market.

I know they're going to want me to say something that incriminates him, but what can I say?

Did he raise him from the dead on the Sabbath? No.

Did he get him to eat anything once he was alive before he'd washed his hands in the way prescribed by the Law? No.

Did he become ritually unclean by touching Lazarus while he was still dead? No.

I suppose I could say that he broke the law of death. But then again, I don't think there's a penalty for that.

The Crucifixion of the Lord of Glory

These monologues consider the scripture 'None of the rulers of this age understood it, for if they had, they would not have crucified the Lord of glory' (1 Corinthians 2:8) from the point of view of the speakers who were caught up in these events of eternal significance.

43 A Levite who witnessed the tearing of the curtain in the Temple

BACKSTORY

Benjamin's neighbour: 'I've never seen Ben like this before. He's usually so calm, so composed. He's a decent, rational young man. And he's always been very sociable. Until now. In the last 24 hours he's completely changed. He just wanders around, looking really shocked and scared. He won't say anything to anyone. He doesn't really look at you any more. It's as though he is always looking past you. Something's really shaken him up. I saw a man once who had just nearly drowned in a boating accident. But even he didn't look this bad. It's as if he's in a daze. Or worse. He keeps muttering to himself, but I haven't managed to get near enough to hear what he's saying.'

The incident referred to here gets a single verse in three of the Gospels: Matthew 27:51, Mark 15:38 and Luke 23:45.

MONOLOGUE

[Benjamin is a nervous young man, very jittery. He needs to pace the floor during this monologue.]

It doesn't matter which way I think about it. It must mean something.

I have heard a story about this sort of thing before. But I never really believed it. But now I am not so sure. No, that didn't sound right. 'I used to be uncertain, but now I am not so sure.' Oh, I don't know!

And that's the problem. I just don't know. I mean, nothing prepares you for a thing like this.

I always thought that I had it all figured out, till this week. I knew exactly what I thought, exactly what I believed.

I mean, I am a Levite. One of God's chosen. A servant of God in his own Temple. Surely, if something was going to happen I would have known! I'd heard about the rabble-rouser, but I hadn't actually gone to listen to him. I mean, why would you? Most of the Sanhedrin hadn't clapped eyes on him till the other night. If our leaders choose not to see him, who am I to disagree?

And then he caused a riot, right here in God's house. God can't have wanted that. Can he?

Actually, I didn't agree with what they did next. You don't collaborate with the Romans. We don't betray any of our people to Gentiles. It made me ashamed. But then again, he shouldn't have done it. He even said he would destroy the Temple and make a new one. In three days. Of course, I never actually heard that myself. But I saw the witnesses who said they did hear him. Can't say as I liked the look of them, if the truth be known.

So how is anyone supposed to know anything? I had it all figured out till this week. Supposing he never said that. Or supposing he did. What does it mean? Perhaps this is the start of it. It's never happened before. Curtains don't tear themselves. And I watched it happen. I thought I was going to die. By rights, I should be dead now. I just don't know what to believe.

Get a grip! What do I know for sure?

OK. First, I know what I saw. It went dark. In the middle of the day. Not cloudy, but black. Pitch black. For hours. And then suddenly it was light.

Then, the curtain ripped. From top to bottom. The curtain that shields us from the most holy place ripped. Ripped in two. Right in half. That curtain has been there for hundreds of years. It's there for a reason. When priests go behind that curtain, they wear a bell and a rope. If they die, we're meant to pull them out. They say that, before I was born, an angel was seen in the Temple once. The man who saw him didn't speak for nearly a year. I've met people who knew him.

The trouble is, my mind keeps wandering. Stick to the facts! The things you actually saw, not what anyone else said.

Facts. It was a normal day. And then it went black. And about three hours later suddenly it was light. And the curtain ripped. Like someone had had enough of it. That's it. Like someone wanted it out of the way.

But that curtain is sacred. It separates men from the most holy presence of God. No one could wish it any different. That'd be blasphemy.

That rabble-rouser was being put to death at the same time. I saw him earlier today. I was on my way into the Temple. The Romans had him. They must have tortured him for hours. He could hardly walk. Someone else had to carry the wood that they were going to nail him to.

All this can't be connected, can it? Three days. That's what he said. Something would happen in three days. Well, that's it, then.

Just wait. If nothing earth-shattering happens in three

days, then all this is just coincidence. Natural phenomena. If something does happen, well – who knows? Everything may change. I mean everything. If God doesn't want that curtain any more, it means he's going to live out here. With us.

Three days. OK. Let's see.

44 Malchus

BACKSTORY

The Kidron Valley is the ravine that separates the Temple Mount and the City of David on the west from the Mount of Olives on the east. An ephemeral stream flows through it, and occasionally it even has flash floods. 'Kidron' means dusky or gloomy. This valley, with its shadows and sinister overtones, was the venue for the most cowardly betrayal and the most wicked arrest in history. Reading John 18:1–12 will give you the background.

MONOLOGUE

Don't look at me – I can't tell you anything.

Well, obviously I was there. And yes, it was me that got into that fight. Undignified, and unprofessional. But the fracas certainly wasn't of my making. And its resolution was bizarre.

The problem was. . . The thing is. . . No. Let me start at the start.

My name is Malchus. I'm a Temple servant. And not just any Temple servant. I am servant to the high priest. This certainly wasn't my normal work. But then again, this Jesus wasn't exactly a run-of-the-mill problem.

Oh, the words he spoke to the populace were full of

charm and radiance, bringing to the fore that unique take of his on how God was accessible to ordinary folk. And while we at the Temple may have cringed at the emphasis, we would not have made a public issue of it.

No, it was his words concerning us, phrases such as 'They are full of greed and self-indulgence' and 'They do not practise what they preach', and even comparing us to 'unmarked graves, which men walk over without knowing it'. This kind of assault on our status and standing in society amounted to a kind of iconoclasm which would have been damaging to society had we allowed it to continue unchecked.

So I'm sure that any thinking man could see we had to do something. Deciding precisely what has been harder. I know some who felt that the man could be reasoned with, persuaded to tone down the rhetoric. I, for one, doubt that such a course of action would have got us anywhere useful.

Not that I was entirely sure at first of the wisdom of the course we did follow, but it gained a momentum of its own and in the end attained a kind of inevitability.

Still, forming a crowd with a Roman guard was an entirely uncomfortable experience. But when we got to the olive grove where he was, most of my doubts were dispelled. I had feared that this could turn into the kind of fiasco we have witnessed in the past, where the men sent to arrest him applaud him instead, returning with empty hands and all too often empty heads, muttering something like 'No one ever spoke the way this man does.'

But today the arrest was at least successful, if somewhat muddled. It was made easier by finding his companions clutching swords and bags of money, looking like any other gang of cut-throats.

After that, it became more chaotic.

We had, so to speak, a man on the inside, Judas. He knew where the grove was that they had often been to in the past. When we got there, this Jesus was speaking to his followers, and Judas approached him as though to greet him, but Jesus asked him, 'Judas, are you betraying the Son of Man with a kiss?'

It was fairly obvious that something was up. He couldn't have missed the rest of us, with our lights and swords, and he turned to us and said, 'Who is it you want?'

The guards seemed a bit caught out by this, and even more caught out by his readiness to give himself up. In fact he had to say it twice, adding, 'If you are looking for me, then let these men go.'

When his friends realised what was happening, one of them lunged at me. I felt an excruciating pain on the side of my head, and there was bucket-loads of blood. When I put my hand to the cut, my whole ear had been severed and was just hanging on by a piece of skin.

And then a strange thing happened. This Jesus was looking more frustrated than aggressive and called out, 'No more of this! Put your sword away!'

And he touched my face. The pain stopped, and when I put my hand to the place again my ear was restored. Don't ask me how. There were still considerable amounts of blood on me, on my assailant and on the ground, but when I felt my face, there wasn't even a scratch.

Now suddenly he was angry and rounded on us. 'Am I leading a rebellion? Is that why you have come with swords and clubs? Every day I was with you in the Temple courts, and you did not lay a hand on me.'

And then he added, 'But this is your hour – when darkness reigns.'

To be honest, I think it would have been difficult to do anything other than what we did. But when he said that, it did seem to make what we were doing look bleak, and the whole situation suddenly seem to fill with foreboding.

45 Joseph of Arimathea

BACKSTORY

Joseph of Arimathea was a Sadducee. The average reader of the Gospels will be familiar with the Pharisees. With their many and often convoluted rules, and their belief that these rules were every bit as binding as the written Law of God, they were often seen as holy men by the common people. The Sadducees, however, considered only the first five books of the Bible as authoritative, and hence they didn't believe in many of the spiritual insights given in the rest of the Old Testament, like the resurrection. They were a smaller movement, centred mainly in Jerusalem, far more wealthy and powerful than the Pharisees, but they had no real following among the populace.

The Gospels tell us that Joseph was a disciple of Jesus, but in secret, because he feared the Jews (John 19:38), and that he was a good and upright man, who had not consented to the Council of Israel's decision and action (Luke 23:50–51).

MONOLOGUE

At the moment, the only thing we can be sure of is that everything is in doubt.

I have never lived through a period like this before, when

the leadership of the nation was in such a poor state and subject to such unrealistic alliances. This Jesus appears to have done the impossible: uniting Pharisees, Sadducees and Herodians, at least in opposition to him. Genuine statesmanship, let alone genuine godliness, seems in very short supply right now.

It appears that many have detached their God-given leadership from any sense of responsibility to the God who gave it. I appreciate that we in the Council of Israel are in the unhappy position of being leaders but not rulers. Our authority is considerably curtailed by the Romans, meaning that we give the impression that our leadership is exercised by their will, rather than the will of God. And how have we responded to this? At the moment, it would appear that we have connived to get their approval for a course of action which I am convinced does not have the approval of God.

A man has appeared in our society who himself does have all the hallmarks of having the approval of God. He has famously denounced many in leadership for their legalism and vainglorious style. In this he has won the admiration of many of the common people, but also implacable enmity from a number of people in high places. More importantly, and more worryingly, I believe that in this matter he expressed the heart of our God.

The shameful scheming of my colleagues has cast our entire claim to legitimacy into serious doubt. We have made ourselves no better than the Romans we claim to despise by conspiring and collaborating with them to destroy the man Jesus, who may even have been correct in his assertion that God intends to shake our old order out of its complacency.

What do we have to fear? Many in the Council have said that we could lose our Temple and our very nationhood if

Jesus' teaching were to take hold. I for one cannot imagine that this is true. In reality we were losing face, nothing more than losing face. Our shortcomings were being held up to the light, and this was being done in a very public arena. Suggesting otherwise and seeking to justify what we have done by claiming that the security of the nation was at risk is nothing short of the most shameful political posturing. We have spun a web of deceit and sought to use it to suppress the truth about what we have done.

Let us not underestimate the enormity of this matter. We have killed an innocent man. Not only that, but we did it in a most cowardly fashion, handing him over to Gentiles so that they could torture him to death. We have let the gutters run with his blood. But it didn't just fill the gutters. It spilled over into our lives. No one walks away from this blameless. No one. In heart, we were all there.

For now, all that I can do is condemn this heinous activity, even if in so doing I convict myself. Till now I have always been proud of my heritage as a Sadducee. The movement came by its name from Zadok, the greatest priest who ever lived. We glory in our history. God has given us the Temple, the Law, the land and this state. It is true that Sadducee teaching reaches only a few men, but it is no coincidence that those men hold the highest offices in the land. We have numbered among our ranks many of the good and the great of Israel. We have not been a movement of the people in the same way as the Pharisees. We have not indulged in the kind of popular personalising of religion and law that they do, and I have always seen that as one of our strengths.

That is, until recently. Jesus' oratory has shaken my beliefs to their core.

For him, the faith was neither a matter of statehood, as we say, nor one of personal law-keeping, as the Pharisees say. He spoke of God as though he knew him. It never occurred to me before that a man could know God, and even now it seems outrageous. If it were to be true, then my whole world would be built on a false premise. But inside I feel unable to resist the appeal of it. To know God. The magnitude of it is matched only by the simplicity of the way he taught it. I'm not sure I can believe it, but I certainly can't forget it.

I have one thing which I can do to ensure that something decent can come from all this blood-letting. I have never believed in life after death, although I know that Jesus did. What I believe is that there should be dignity after death. In the fashion of many Sadducees and others of wealth and standing I have a tomb which is prepared for me when I die. But if we don't challenge the behaviour of the Romans, they won't even bury Jesus. I can't accept that his body should be treated in this way. And I don't expect Pilate to want any further controversy.

Jesus was a foot or so taller than me, and so today I have sent a stone mason to my tomb to make the space for the body longer. I intend to ask Pilate to release the body to my care, and I will have him buried in the tomb where I intended to be buried myself.

Some accounts have been circulating that he claimed he would rise from the dead. I have never believed in any kind of resurrection. But the Council are going to insist that the body is closely guarded to prevent spurious claims. They may even ask the Romans to provide the guard. So be it. At least this way we can show him proper respect.

But these are things that we need not concern ourselves

with. I am not expecting anything, and I am certain that a following that shared his love of truth will not be faking anything. And, of course, if God does surprise us all and something inconceivable were to occur, we would not be able to prevent it, even should a whole Roman legion be deployed to guard the tomb.

Do I believe that he will rise from the dead? Of course not. But it's like his assertion that you can know God. I'm not sure I can believe it, but I certainly can't forget it.

46 The centurion

BACKSTORY

The centurion: 'This would not be my first choice for a post-ing. In fact, it wouldn't even be my last choice. If I could, I would resign my commission. I have fought the barbarians knowing that if I lose I could be hacked to death. No chance of that here. But there is a serious risk of being bored to death. Nothing ever seems to happen. These people wran-gle over how long the tassels should be on their robes, or whether home-grown herbs have to be given to their god. They are the most legalistic people I have ever encountered. But what can I do? I came out of our last battle too crippled to ever fight again. So I am posted to this backwater. And for all I know, I will never see any kind of action again.'

The incidents referred to in this monologue can be found in Mark 12:13–17 and 15:15–39.

MONOLOGUE

[He is seated at a table]

Come in, come in! Shut the door! No, I'm not afraid. Well, I am, but not in the way you think. You want an explana-tion for the events of the last few days. You are not alone. I have already had messengers from the Council of Israel and a surreptitious enquiry from Pilate's own household. Listen, a week ago I hadn't even heard of this man. Of course I'm sure!

[Gets up. Walks with a stick, owing to a noticeable limp]

Ten days ago, I received orders to put the guard from the Fortress of Antonia on alert. A rabble-rouser from the north, a Galilean, was expected in Jerusalem – an unpredictable and enigmatic man, by all accounts, and with a large following. The instructions came from Pilate. Although I have only lived here two years, I grow weary of the constant state of turmoil in which these people seem to live. This is the high spot of their year. Passover. It is a celebration of when they escaped from the slave masters of Egypt. There is always a danger that they will draw parallels with our Roman Empire.

A week ago, I took a stroll from the fortress through the tunnel to the Temple. Yes, they only have one Temple – and they're quite precious about it. They believe their god lives there, and foreigners are only allowed into the outer court. It's a stinking animal market, and not an experience I recommend. This time, I was just there to check for trouble. In front of me, sat on the floor, was a large man. He had collected some cords from the floor and was plaiting them together. Reminded me of watching fishermen at the docks in Rome splicing rope. Very meticulous. I would say he was either a craftsman or a fisherman. He looked preoccupied, and for that moment I dismissed him as a harmless eccentric and walked on. The next thing I knew there was an almighty commotion. I turned to see that the man had finished his cord work and was using it as a primitive whip. He had lifted the huge oak money-table in the centre of the courtyard and thrown it into the animal pen. He must have had the strength of an ox. Now he was using his whip to drive the animals from the broken pen. All the time he was calling out things like 'How dare you!' and 'My Father has not given permission for this!' He was magnificent. Before I was invalided out of active service **[he indicates the stick]** I'd fought on the battlefields of Europe with some of the best warriors of Rome. But I have never seen a man like this before. His appearance was ordinary, but his commanding presence was something to see. Then, suddenly, he stopped, sat down on one of the remaining tables and began to speak. From his accent I would say he was a Galilean.

Something about prayer, and this being his Father's house, the only court where foreigners could come to pray. He looked right at me when he said that bit. He asked why they were using this precious space as a market. Then someone called out, 'If you are against greed, why should we pay taxes to greedy Romans?' The Galilean asked to borrow a coin. Someone offered him a Roman denarius. He held it up and said, 'Whose image is stamped on the coin?' Everyone called out 'Caesar's', and some of them spat. He just smiled. 'Then give it to Caesar. Your hearts were stamped in the image of God, so give them to God.' I left. The man may have been a threat to the Council of Israel, but he appeared to be no threat to Rome.

The next I knew of him was a few days later when I got an early morning summons to Pilate's residence. It appears the Galilean had been arrested after all. By the time I got there, Pilate had obviously had the man severely beaten, and there was a major altercation going on between Pilate and the Council. They wanted the Galilean crucified for claiming to be God's Son. Pilate disagreed, but in the end he conceded. He is so weak. I mean, has he no respect for his own men? I have never believed crucifying villains was a job fit for a Roman soldier. Actually, crucifixion is not a job fit for any man. It is a vicious and cowardly way to end a man's life. When I signed up for the army of Rome, I was thinking of all the stories we heard as children of courage and honour. I am a soldier, not a pacifist. I am not afraid to fight, nor ashamed to kill in battle. But crucifixion is no battle. It needs no courage, and it strips you of your own honour. But this was worse even than that. It was clear to anyone who cared to look that the man was no threat to Rome. He had committed no crime against the peace of Rome. But Pilate was too busy with his political manoeuvring.

The two rookie soldiers I took with me had never done a crucifixion before. At least they gave the first two criminals some drugged wine. It stupefies the victims and makes the whole thing easier. Nevertheless, the first man kept struggling and cursing, and the lads covered up their inexperience with excessive brutality. The second thief just wept. When they came to him, he fell on his knees. Offered money, even offered his own family. I tell you, it is no job fit for a Roman soldier, dealing with this kind of vermin. Then they came to the Galilean, and I thought: 'This is going to get out of hand.' I had seen him in action in the Temple. He refused the wine, even when one of them shouted at him, 'Just drink it!' Then the other one barked at him, 'Get on the floor!' – and he did. Again he shouted, 'Get on the wood!' – and he did. Everyone was awestruck. He offered no resistance at all. Even when they took his hand to nail it, he didn't try to fight. He just looked at them and said, 'Father, they don't know what they are doing.' Well, I've already told you that they didn't know what they were doing, but I don't think he meant it like that. I think he was praying, but he sounded so sure of who he was talking to that the men looked round for his father. Of course there was no one there. Then he said, 'Father, forgive them.' After that, one of the lads couldn't finish the job. I had to hold the nails. It turned my stomach. I kept thinking, 'I will never forgive Pilate for this.' Then I remembered the Galilean praying forgiveness for the lads, and then I didn't know what to think. We always keep some undrugged wine for the soldiers. After the crosses were up, all of us belted back enough to relieve the shock. I kept wondering if the Galilean's prayer included me. Do you think he was forgiving me too?

For the next few hours nothing much happened. Crucifixion is a very slow way to die. Usually you suffocate when you can't push your body up enough to get a breath, but it can take days. The crowd threw the usual insults and then began to disperse. The lads played a game of dice for the Galilean's robe. And me? I just stood there.

Then suddenly it started. Within minutes a fearsome wind began that seemed to blow away the sun and all the light. You must have seen the darkness, but it was worse outside the city. It was worst near him. No one had a torch. It was so dark that you couldn't see your own hand. And the wind was so hot as it hurled sand into our faces that it was hard for us to breathe. I can't imagine what it must have been like for them. And then there was an acrid sulphurous smell, and I had a rancid taste in my mouth. I could hear one of the lads being sick, but no one spoke. I thought I could hear occasional insane laughter and deathly screams, but it might have just been the wind. As the hours dragged on, I wondered if it would ever end. I have come out of some vicious battles and said that I had been through hell, but this – this really was hell. Suddenly I was overcome with a fear like iced water running through my veins. If he was someone special, maybe a mystic with unknown powers or even God's Son like he had claimed, what then? What had we done? Was he even still there? Had he left, gone to his kingdom and abandoned the whole world to this filthy darkness? Perhaps this was the end. How long would it be before we would all fall on our own swords? What if everyone had gone, and he had left me alone to face this by myself? What if I was alone? Did his prayer include me? Was he going to forgive me? What if I couldn't even die? What if this went on for ever? Don't look at me as if you think I'm mad – you weren't there!

Then I heard him call. At least he was still there. I wanted to run to him, but I still couldn't see. He called to his God, saying, 'Why did you abandon me?' No. I don't know what he meant. Surely *we* were the God-forsaken ones. Then the light began to break, and the wind dropped. I looked up at the crosses and saw that the other two were nearly unconscious, but he was looking at us. He was drenched in sweat and blood, and looked like a man emerging from the theatre of war. I remembered how he had looked at me a week ago, saying that I should have gone to his Father's house to pray. Who is his Father? Was he really God's Son? Then he shouted, 'It is finished.' For a second I thought he meant that *he* was finished. But it was no despairing cry. It sounded like a victorious one. And when I looked at him, his beaten face radiated elation – like a soldier returning home, or a bridegroom on his way to the wedding. Then he just died. I cried out something like, 'He was God's Son. He was God's Son,' but it was too late. He was dead.

Since then I have been in a kind of daze. I can't eat. I can't sleep. I have slept like a baby on the day before a battle, but not now. Who was he? What have I done? Last night I dozed at one point and woke up to find I was crying. Not quiet weeping, but convulsed in fierce tears and sobs. What have I done?

And now the Council have sent word to me that they don't think he was really dead. They think he must have escaped from the tomb, because he has been seen walking near the city. Of course he was dead. Even if he hadn't died, you wouldn't have seen him walking, not today. After all that was done to him that day he'd probably never walk again. Of course he was dead.

And I was wrong. He is a threat to the Roman Empire. He's more than a threat to the Roman Empire. He is its nemesis. Somehow he had something to do with that darkness. If he chooses to let it return, we are all lost. And as for the Council, they can try to hush this up all they want. It isn't going to go away. He isn't going to go away. Somehow he has come back from the most unimaginable death. And I, for one, intend to try to find him, although I have no idea how. I keep hearing his voice in my head saying, 'Father, forgive them,' and I need to know if he would be willing to include me in that prayer. The truth is, I still don't know what it all means. I still don't know what I should do.

Do you?

47 Zacchaeus

BACKSTORY

Zacchaeus's neighbour: 'I have to say, I was shocked when I saw Jesus going to Zacchaeus's house. We have always seen Zacchaeus as the worst kind of opportunist and traitor. He fancies himself as a businessman, but he has grown rich by colluding with the Roman army. They made him rich. That and helping himself at our expense. Not that the Roman bully-boys cared. I can't see Jesus managing to explain this. It'll kill his reputation, even among those convinced that God was with him.'

Reading Luke 19:1–10 will give you the background to this story.

MONOLOGUE

I am the man that Jesus chose to spend one of his last few days with before he was killed. It's the most significant thing about me.

Sure there are other things about me you should know, but none that defines me as much as that day.

For instance, I am the man who lives in the biggest house on the edge of town. You must have seen it. And I was the shortest kid of his age in the entire town of Jericho; the one

that got teased and bullied for being so little. Then I became
the most successful entrepreneur in the town, if you equate
affluence with success. On the other hand, if you equate
popularity with success, I was the most miserable failure in
the town.

You have probably already decided what sort of man I
am. That's OK. You pays your money and you takes your
choice. And whoever you paid your money to, it doesn't
matter. They all worked for me.

And me? I worked for the Romans.

So who am I? Well, as I said before, I am the man that
Jesus chose to spend one of his last few days with before he
was killed. That's who. And that day is now carved into my
consciousness and will, for the rest of my life, be a haunt-
ing, overbearing memory that imposes its life on any lesser
imaginations or ambitions that I once had. And I wouldn't
have it any other way. That is to say, that day meant so
much, if anything means anything any more, that is.

I wasn't born rich. In fact, I nearly wasn't born at all.
Everyone says I was born early, the runt of the litter. A very
sickly little child who grew up to be a disappointment. 'No
identifiable skills,' as one of the rabbis put it, explaining to
my parents why he couldn't see anyone wanting me as an
apprentice. Fair enough, really. I challenge anyone to take
a good look at my old man and identify any skills there
either. You could say that indolence ran in our family.
Although it didn't actually run. It just kind of moseyed
along.

At that time the Romans were looking for locals they
could use to collect taxes. It seemed like easy money. Everyone had to pay and any defaulters got reported by me to the
garrison. Getting a visit from a Roman squaddie could put

the wind up anyone, so no one took the risk. All I had to do was hint at a visit and people paid up. Even if I had added a bit to the bill. 'Z rate', I called it. A bit extra for your old friend Zacchaeus. And people paid it.

Of course, I haven't had to do that for years. Haven't had to deal with the punters at all. Got people to do all that for me. The Romans' real trick was always to get someone with enough local knowledge and enough nous to get the whole operation running smoothly. So I stepped up to the challenge. And I haven't needed to get my hands dirty for years. Just watched as the money came in.

But Jesus had a whole different way to see life. He said it wasn't at all a question of who we should pay taxes to. He showed me that life wasn't about money, or Romans, or nationalistic pride, or taxes.

It's not even about us.

It is all about God with his zeal for people, his plan and preparation for our lives, his infatuation with us and our unfolding narratives, his passion to find us in all our brokenness and restore us to himself.

After Jesus had finished, all I could think about was how much I had got wrong, and how unlikely it was that God would be interested in what was left of my life. But Jesus said he was, and he seemed to know him so well.

No one ever accused me of too much premeditation, and that day was no exception.

'Right now,' I shouted, 'right now I am giving half of my possessions to the poor. And anyone I have ever cheated I will repay four times over. Right now. Come on.'

What a rush. It felt so liberating. And he welcomed me to God's family. I felt so loved.

A few days later he was dead, murdered by my employers,

the Romans, in league with my sworn enemies, the Council of Israel.

I don't know what happens next. We are here in our chaos, and we have butchered the only man who really seemed to know the way out. Somehow we were all in the middle, somewhere in between the extremes of that unholy alliance.

How is it that anyone can think that God is more interested in who collects duty than who distributes pity, in censuring the enemies of state than ensuring justice for his friends? But his killers covered the whole gamut of persuasion, race and human behaviour. Like I said, we were all in there somewhere.

And now, we are all left stuck in the crippling, stultifying maze that gets called 'normality'.

They say that he brought a man back from the dead in Bethany. Everyone was talking about it. That's why I wanted to see him. But it's crazy even to talk like this now.

I can't really have reached 35 and all the time have misunderstood the very nature of the world this much – or can I? It's unthinkable.

Yet I can't believe he's gone. How could it be possible for such an indefatigable life to be defeated by that degree of evil chaos? It isn't really feasible that a life like his could ever end.

Maybe the unthinkable is our only hope of sanity.

The Resurrection

48 One of the bribed guards

Another guard: 'I was one of the four assigned to the "quaternion", the four Roman soldiers designated by Pilate to guard the tomb. An easy job that has turned into my worst nightmare. If we say we all fainted, we will be put on a charge, possibly even executed. If we say, as we have been told to, that we were asleep on duty and our governor hears about it, we will also be put on a charge and, maybe, executed. But at least this way we have someone who says they will keep us out of the mire if things go belly-up. And if we get away with it, we will have come out of this with the tidy sum we have been given to tell the "fell asleep on duty" story. But I still wish it had never happened.'

Reading Matthew 27:62–28:15 will give you the background to this story.

MONOLOGUE

OK. So we didn't actually see it. I suppose in a strict sense we lied. But wouldn't you, faced with what we're faced with? And anyway, it was only a lie in the strictly technical sense that we didn't actually see any of the things we swore that we had seen. But they must have happened. The alternative was just so. . . Well, there isn't really an alternative.

It's really simple. We got a job: 'Guard this dead body and don't let it go anywhere.' How hard could that be? The only drawback was there's a group of so-called insurgents known as 'the Disciples' who could try to steal it over the next few days. And, sure enough, the body went missing. So it must have been 'the Disciples'. Right?

Of course it's right. And make no mistake – the one I saw must easily have been eight feet. And this is where it gets complicated. . .

He didn't really look. . . Well, he didn't really look human. . . At all.

Now of course that's not possible. I know we Romans have a whole pantheon of gods, and this lot in Jerusalem could only manage one, but the point is we don't really think of our gods as real. Not in the sense of. . . well. . . real. Like they could do anything physical. I know some Romans do believe in them, but that's just 'cos they're sentimental or superstitious. Now this lot in Jerusalem do believe that the one god they've actually got is real. But they also believe he won't do anything without their approval.

And posting an armed guard over a dead body to stop it getting away is a fair old clue that they disapprove. Of course we all knew he was dead. I mean, come on! We're the Roman army – the most efficient killing machine in the world. We've got gladiators to strike fear into the boldest heart. I think we can tackle a peace-loving carpenter with only a bunch of yellow-livered friends as allies – come on!

No, we all knew that we had done our usual job of killing. Smash them up and then beat them down. That's what I say. He wasn't going anywhere. Leastwise not on his own!

And that was what was worrying these Jerusalem boys.

They thought his yellow-livered friends might get a sudden rush of blood to the head and try to steal his body. That'd be a turn-up for the books, doing a jail break on a dead man. Apparently the carpenter had said he would rise from the dead. But we're the Romans. When we do a job – well, let's just say you won't need a money-back guarantee.

No, as I said earlier, they thought that this rag-bag set of washouts, instead of all running away at the mere sight of one of us with a sword, might turn insurgents and try to steal the body and then say that he had got up all by himself.

Now it could be that there is no word in Hebrew for 'gullible', but no one is going to believe he's got himself alive again unless he turns up. Maybe invites a few hundred people to an 'I'm alive again' party or maybe goes fishing with his mates, something like that. And we all know that's not going to happen.

So, from my point of view this job was a breeze, almost an insult. Guard a man who was already dead from a bunch of cowards who might as well be. It was a tough assignment. It was going to take guts. There are only a few men who can handle something that demanding. And they're called. . . only absolutely any dumb soldier in the army, that's who!

So what went wrong? Truth is, I don't really know.

There was definitely an earthquake. Everyone in the entire city knows that. And I mean an earthquake. Not a tremor – a quake. Some of the buildings in the area have been devastated, and there are all kinds of reports of weird goings-on that night. Well, we can be fairly sure that these 'Disciples' didn't do that.

I think it was just a very unfortunate coincidence. It certainly added to the confusion of that night, and could actually provide an explanation. I'm not quite sure what explanation, but given enough time I'm sure we could come up with one. It's what happened next that I don't have an explanation for. Nor does anyone else. And I've been given a serious wad of cash to keep this bit hush. Suits me. Nothing but trouble can come out of this for all of us, so keeping it hush suits me fine.

You remember me saying that one of them didn't look human and that he was huge? Well, there's a bit more. He was a lightning man. Seriously, the only time I have seen a light that bright it was lightning. But this guy was covered in it, like he'd stepped straight out of a bolt of lightning. I mean his clothes were like snow they were so white, but his skin and his hair – lightning. He glowed. He actually blazed. Like walking fire.

Sure I've been afraid before, though I wouldn't tell that to anyone else. But you're bound to get the odd twinge when you're called out to a province where there's been an uprising and you're sent out to a fight to the death with some insurrectionist army.

But this went beyond any fear. This guy could have killed us by looking at us. But he didn't. Instead, he smiled the most gracious smile you've ever seen, like he was on our side. Then he put just one hand on the stone that we had all struggled to roll across the mouth of the tomb only two days ago and he rolled it right back. And then he jumped up and sat on it.

And then I must have passed out, but when I came to, the body was gone. I tell you, if this gets out, nothing but trouble can come of it.

49 The traveller on the Emmaus road

BACKSTORY

The traveller's wife: 'I always thought his parents chose his name wisely: Ittamar, island of palms. That's just what he's like, an island – hard to get to sometimes, but always tranquil. Always, except for those few days last year, that is. He saw it all, all except the final killing. He's normally the sort who'd turn away from any kind of violence. And when he came home that night, he was. . . well, I suppose you'd call it traumatised. He just sat, sometimes motionless, sometimes shaking and crying. I know he was scared and worried that if they started rounding up the others and he was identified, then I could be caught up in it as well. I think that's why he thought it best if he went away with Cleopas for a few days; away where no one could recognise him. But neither of us bargained on what happened next. . . '

Reading Luke 24:13–35 will give you the background to this story.

MONOLOGUE

I don't think I have ever had all my feelings just go missing before. To have given up on life for ever as the sun rises, to have actually prayed the night before that you wouldn't have to wake up again, to feel so far adrift from all you had believed was real that nothing really connects, to feel yourself wondering if you have inadvertently gone mad and think that you can never know for sure. . . This is the darkness that enveloped me.

Where do I start? To begin at the beginning seems ludicrous. At the beginning my world was safe, predictable, with the kind of certainties that could easily slip into comfortable repetitiveness. Sure I had my plans, but they were about extending the farm and building a family. I had only been married two years, it was not yet a year since my father had died, and I had inherited his farm and all his business. My life was comfortable, mapped out, and I was at ease. And if I had never met *him*, I could have lived that way, slipping into a kind of amorphous oblivion, living with an ill-defined sense of purpose and probably dying in a similarly indistinct fashion. But I did meet him, with his gentle way of instituting personal crisis in all who met him, with his unfathomable sense of destiny and his unassuming way of introducing revolutionary ideas as though they were self-evident.

And I fell in love. In love with his God, with his message, with everything about him. He became my all, the touchstone for my life, its foundation and capstone. I thought he was the Christ. In the end it became inconceivable that he wasn't. We rarely spoke of it, but Peter once told him that he believed that he was the Christ. Jesus told him never to speak of it again until he rose from the dead, but we had no more understanding of his meaning than if he had said not to speak of it until all the sea rose to the sky.

We weren't expecting his arrest. He told us to expect it, and it wasn't that we didn't believe him. We simply didn't understand him, couldn't conceive how the man that we all quietly believed was the Messiah could be arrested.

I wasn't there when he was arrested. Apparently it was a shambles. Despite having a traitor on hand to identify him, they still weren't sure. And when he confidently identified himself as the man they sought, it shocked them into total disarray. He could have simply strolled through their midst. He'd done it before. But instead he waited patiently while they picked themselves up and regained their composure, indulging this bungling attempt at arrest. He permitted them to apprehend him and take him to what they laughingly described as a trial. And from what I hear, he was in control of the whole fiasco.

What happened next was ugly, monstrous, hideous. I hesitate to even speak of it. They behaved as if they had caught the most odious felon themselves, instead of having a good man come to them freely.

What they did to him was horrifying, foul. They got the Romans to do what they would never have done themselves. They think they have kept their self-righteous souls clear of the obscenities of that day. In reality, one way or another the blood of that day will never leave them. In a way I don't think it will really leave any of us.

I watched what those butchers did for hours, till they took him off to die. I couldn't watch that.

I joined a few of the others. And we wept and screamed and then sat in numbed silence for hours. In the end Cleopas and I decided to try leaving the city. It was risky. We weren't sure if they were going to start rounding us all up for similar treatment, but I couldn't stand that deafening, deadening quiet any more, so we left, slipping quietly out of the gate before the streets were busy.

But that silence followed us, stalking us down the lanes, confronting us with the awful event at every step; so it was a strange relief when a stranger fell in alongside us. He seemed unaware of all that had just occurred.

Just before we left, strange reports began to reach us that his body had gone missing, and there was some talk of angels and wild claims that he was alive.

But when we told this stranger all that we had seen and heard, including these bizarre narratives, and also all we had hoped for, he laughed and said that we had misunderstood and misconstrued the whole thing – called us foolish and slow. And yet his words were calm and reassuring.

He began at Genesis. God's plan, he said. But not in its entirety. The animal whose skin covered Adam and Eve was the first of many, covering our sin, not solving our problem. From the world's inception all human life has been on a collision course with God's life.

He showed us that at the very start, we were promised an answer to all that the serpent had begun, but it was an answer with a cost. Here, right at the start, the whole of humanity was promised a Messiah who would crush Satan's head, but at a cost. Satan would strike at his heel.

I'd never seen that before. And he went right through the Scriptures, opening book after book, prophecy after prophecy, promise after promise, all saying the same. We approached the village where we were to stay, and he went to take his leave, but we urged him to stay. There seemed so much more that he could tell us. He accepted our offer of a meal, and then he broke bread for us.

And then we knew. That unassuming way of introducing revolutionary ideas as though they were self-evident. I only ever knew one man who could do that; who could bring fresh meaning to every sunrise, fresh cohesion to our lives; who could bring us reality, sanity and hope.

How did I ever believe that mere human bully-boys could extinguish that Light?

50 A witness from Matthew 28

BACKSTORY

There comes a time in the life of most believers when they find their faith stretched to breaking point. The questions can come so thick and fast. Why has this happened? What does it all mean? Where is God? Meet here a man to whom believing that death was not the end seemed impossible. Then meet the God who understood what he was going through. Reading Matthew 28 will give you the background to this story.

MONOLOGUE

When I think of how the day went, I'm almost ashamed. It's obvious now. How could I ever have doubted it?

But I did. I'm not even sure what it was that I doubted. It wasn't really him that I doubted. You can't really doubt him.

He's a man. And the kindest and most straightforward man I ever met. I don't doubt that. And I don't doubt him. For me, meeting him was the first time that I realised that God has a human side; that he talks and converses; that he laughs and cries; that he is tender and compassionate; that he can get angry; but that he's never crotchety and doesn't sulk. He speaks. Jesus called him his Father. And not in some abstract way. With Jesus you really felt that if he went home, it would be to the house where God lives. And he would say something like, 'Hello, Dad. I'm home.' He used to say things like, 'My Father said. . . ', and you knew that he was recounting a conversation that he'd had with God earlier that morning.

And losing that relationship was all just too much for me. Too much. You know. Life. Everything. The whole thing. You must have felt like that sometimes. Well, that's how I felt.

It was as though everything that really mattered had been taken away. Ever felt like that? It's a lonely feeling. And it doesn't really matter if other people, even people you care about, are going through exactly the same thing. The way you feel is too private, too personal, to properly connect it to anyone else.

I know that probably sounds selfish in a way, but it isn't really. Sometimes grief and anxiety can be too much for us. I just. . . just felt too small. I wanted someone to come and take it all away.

Like when you're a little kid and you've hurt yourself. Just telling your mum about what happened seems to start the healing.

Well, now I've grown up. So who do I tell when every-thing gets bent out of shape, when I can't fit my life together any more?

I used to tell him. And he understood. I told him any-thing and everything. If I'd had a row at home, if the crops had got blight, if the local Roman centurion had started throwing his weight around in the village – anything. And just the act of telling him and being with him seemed to start the healing, made me realise that God had an answer.

So what happens if he's gone? There's no one else.

The Romans took him away. And we all went to pieces. He said we would. He said if the shepherd got struck, the sheep would be scattered. Well, he certainly got struck. I was there when he was arrested. At first I thought it might even turn out for the best. Maybe if he squared up to the Romans it would settle everything.

But then it all seemed to go so horribly wrong. It was almost as if he felt he could win only by losing. He didn't even try to do what we all knew he could do. He could have put it all straight so easily, shown the world not to mess with him. But he didn't. For reasons that I'm still not at all sure about, he let them win. Or at least that's how it looked.

And we all got scattered. I got scattered. All over the place. I felt as if I was being thrown in a thousand different directions. One minute I was angry. Then I was distraught. Then angry again. Then scared, very scared. Then confused. How could he have let this happen?

And then the apostles tell us to come to this mountain and everything is supposed to be all right. Just like that.

And then Jesus appeared. At least, I thought it was Jesus. It looked like Jesus as he walked around and greeted people. But I couldn't quite hear what he was saying, and I just wasn't sure. I mean, I'm just not used to meeting people after they've died. I know that Jesus could do things like that. I've seen him do it a couple of times. And you could understand it, because it was him that made it happen. But how does that work when you've lost him? How does anything work?

And then he spoke. To all of us. And I thought he might be angry with me. But he wasn't that way at all.

He said, 'All power is given to me.' And immediately I

was sure. It was him. Only he talks like that, with that presence and that authority. It was as though a mist that had been over my mind had suddenly lifted. I have wondered since how it had ever settled on me and not on some of the others. But that's an idle thought. What matters is that he lifted it.

And he said he had a job for us to do. For all of us to do. He didn't exclude me. He didn't send me away for doubting. He wants me. He wants me still. 'Go into all the world,' he said, 'and tell them.'

And suddenly I understood. Only by taking the worst that the world could throw at him could he prove that he could beat it. I suppose if he simply had never died we would have admired him for cheating death. But now he has died, and come back, everyone can see that he actually beat death.

The Roman Empire isn't all-powerful. The Council of Israel isn't all-powerful. Even the fact that everyone will die in the end isn't all-powerful. He is.

And just as I thought it couldn't get any better, he spoke again in that low, firm and reassuring manner of his: 'I'm not going to leave you, not abandon you. I am with you. Always.'

Scripture Index

Numbers to the right of the Bible citation refer to the monologue numbers

50 Dramatic Monologues

by Dave Burt

Few forms of communication can be more powerful than the monologue – one person in front of an audience, creating a character, evoking an atmosphere. He or she can narrate a story, describe events, recall dialogue and, most importantly, say openly what they think.

From the man or woman in the street, from the woman at the well to Judas Iscariot, from laughter to tears, from first romance to old age, it's all here – just watch the reaction as your audience opens up and responds.

DAVID BURT is the author of three other drama books: *50 Sketches About Jesus, 25 Sketches About Proverbs* and *50 Dramatised Bible Readings*. Formerly with the Riding Lights theatre company, he is now on the staff team at Cranleigh Baptist Church in Surrey.

Visit www.davidccook.co.uk